T0386529

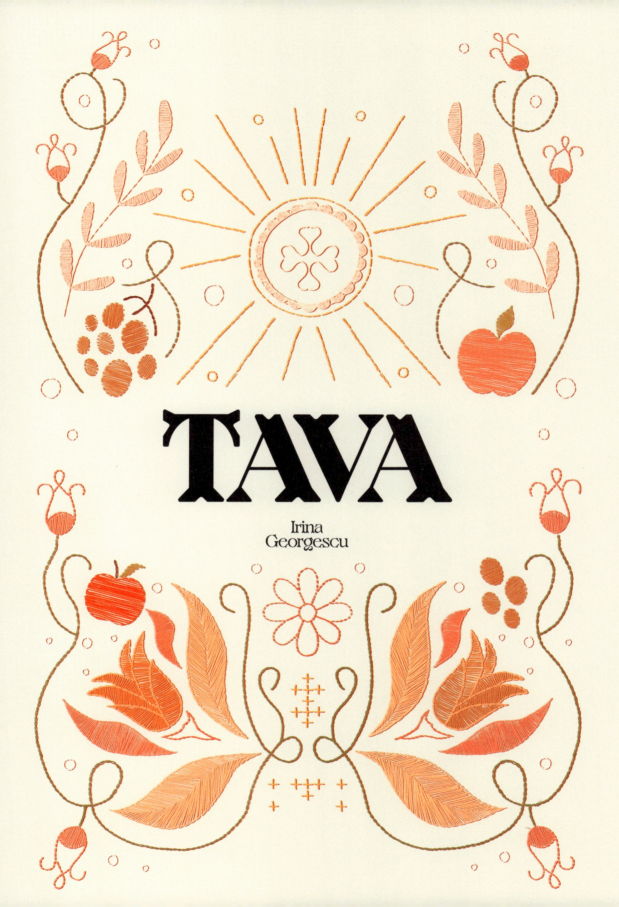

TAVA

Irina
Georgescu

Eastern-European Baking and
Desserts From Romania and Beyond

TAVA

Irina Georgescu

Photography by Matt Russell

Hardie Grant

BOOKS

Introduction 8

'I am such a huge admirer of Irina Georgescu in general, and of this extraordinarily impressive and important book in particular. A must-have, not just for enquiring bakers, but – crucially – for all those interested in the context and evolution of culinary culture.'

Nigella Lawson

'A joy and an education. Irina Georgescu has disentangled the strands woven into Romanian cooking and identity and she has done so deliciously, through glorious cakes, pies, strudels and doughnuts. Cook, eat, learn.'

Diana Henry

Introduction
A constellation of cultures

How we bake in Eastern Europe, and especially in Romania, is largely unknown. My aim in writing this book is to share the stories of those who prepare the dishes that have come to form our national cuisine. These pages contain recipes that speak of the identity of these communities and specific regions across the country. No small task, given that Romania is a constellation of cultures – a 'little Europe', where the Middle East meets Austrian and German influences, layered on top of the inheritance left by the ancient Romans and Greeks. This book is about centuries of diversity and overlapping cultures, from which Romanian cuisine has emerged in all its rich flavours and textures.

I have chosen to focus on just six cultural communities (although there are many more that live in the region) and share their traditions and history through their iconic baking recipes. I couldn't have written a cookery book without this broader context, while still allowing the recipes to take centre stage.

You will find Armenian *pakhlava*, Saxon plum pies, Swabian poppy-seed crescents, Jewish fritters and Hungarian *langoşi* alongside *plăcinte* pies, *alivenci* corn cake, *strudel* and fruit dumplings. Rice or pearl barley puddings, doughnuts and gingerbread biscuits come with their own stories, while chocolate mousses, meringues in custard sauce and coffee ice cream introduce you to the glamour of famous Eastern European pastry shops.

I hope that these recipes will pique your interest and tempt you to embrace the unfamiliar as much as the familiar. Certainly, you will love the comforting and homely feel of all the dishes.

The idea of national cuisine

Romanian cuisine has been influenced over the years by the country's remarkable location within Europe and its impressive topography, dominated by the Carpathian mountains, the Black Sea and the mighty rivers including the Danube, which created regions of flourishing trade with different historical dynamics.

For centuries, the country we know today as Romania was comprised of three main regions: Wallachia in the south, Moldavia in the east and Transylvania, including the neighbouring county Banat, in the centre. The first two were united in 1859, when they freed themselves from the Ottoman Empire and Russian protectorate, while Transylvania and Banat joined in 1918 after the end of the Austro-Hungarian Empire. This is how the cuisines of two empires became part of our national cuisine.

The Republic of Moldova formed later, in 1940, from the historic Romanian principality of Moldavia. It existed for a while as part of the Soviet Union and gained independence only in 1991, retaining Romanian as the official language. In Romania, we refer to both the Republic and the region of Romania by the same name: Moldova.

The first cookbook to use the term 'Romanian', implying a national cuisine, was published in 1865, soon after the first two Romanian principalities had united. The recipes in *Bucătăria română* had been collected by Christ Ionnin from friends, chefs, merchants and intellectuals, and offered a glimpse into what people ate and how they cooked in this newly formed territory. Most of the book reflects a cuisine of the middle classes, strongly influenced by 17th-18th-century western Europe, and is only dotted with Ottoman dishes. It proved how European and how well connected to the Western gastronomic world this new country already was. Ice creams, set creams and soufflés featured heavily in the book, as did puddings involving bread or crushed biscuits cooked with milk, or using bone marrow, almonds and dried fruit, under the name of *turte* or *torte*. Both names described either savoury round flatbreads, or round cakes and puddings. The book also mentioned a variety of doughnuts – fruit dipped in batter then fried; poached fruit such as compotes; *magiun* or *povidlă* plum butter and, not surprisingly, *revani* – Turkish semolina cake.

I find it is difficult to draw a portrait of Romanian cuisine in hard lines – it is more about smooth shading and blending. The many communities here – German, Hungarian, Armenian, Jewish, Turkish, Greek, Ukrainian, Bulgarian, Serbian, Czech, and even French and Italian – brought layer upon layer of influences into Romanian kitchens, which often overlap. Some of these groups were historically prominent and generated various written sources in their own languages, which has made it difficult to trace back or claim any Romanian provenance to dishes.

Any attempt to profile the concept of Romanian cuisine, sooner or later, hits the vast wall of the Communist regime.

Firstly, the massive import of recipes from Western cookery books contributed to the abandonment of many of our regional, characterful foods. The imports were meant to prove that working men and women of a classless society had access to sophisticated foods. Yet it eventually led to a culinary mismatch.

Secondly, in an attempt to bring in hard currency from the western markets through tourism, the regime introduced terms to romanticise the provenance of dishes: recipes would be described as 'shepherds' this', or 'hunters' that'; we see 'hut' cake (the latter a copy of a royal cake called *Caraiman*), *haiduc* grilled chops

(*haiduci* were outlaws, like Robin Hood), or 'gypsy' fillet steak creep in. The regime also standardised cookery books and restaurant menus, and many people today consider those recipes to be 'traditional' and at the core of our national cuisine.

Thirdly, the focus on mono-crops and imports to feed the masses, such as wheat, rice and sunflower (for oil), had a devastating effect on the diversity of our local culinary landscape. It sent many traditional grains and plants into oblivion.

Today, there is a desire to rediscover ingredients and cooking methods from the past, and incorporate them into our modern lives.

Introduction

An intricate fabric

Throughout this book, you will be able to piece together a social and political landscape of some of the regions in Romania, and the relations between their people. You will find the Székelys and the Saxons in south-eastern Transylvania, defending the border at the feet of the Carpathian mountains with their military skills and fortified churches. You will meet the Magyars, the dominant political power of Transylvania, and read about the Swabians in the Banat region of western Romania. I tell the story of the Armenians thriving in an 18th-century cosmopolitan city, which later became the capital of Romania: Bucharest. I talk about the Jewish communities influencing the commercial landscape of Moldavia and the ports on the Danube river in the east. There are stories about Casa Capşa, the iconic pastry shop in Bucharest, and about the Romanian monarchy modernising and uniting the country. The book also encompasses a longer journey from Romania to Hungary and Germany, as the countries have a lot of history in common and, through it, a shared culture, too.

The stories in the book intertwine to weave an intricate fabric of Romanian identity. It is exactly from this interconnection that Romanian cuisine emerges: we are all on the same journey, bringing our own dishes to the table and being fiercely proud of what we have to share.

Since we can't look at Romanian cuisine in isolation, I avoided using the word 'unique' to describe it. I prefer to say 'this is how we eat in Romania' – a kaleidoscope of old, traditional and regional recipes, relevant to who we are now. I wrote the book in appreciation of our rich culinary diversity and heritage, which is slowly starting to be restored. Many recipes follow the traditional ways, keeping loyal to the original textures and flavours of the dishes, with the occasional element that celebrates the culinary folklore around them.

Flavours

Throughout the book, I use ingredients that are readily available
in supermarkets, international food shops or online.
Nothing is out of reach or season nowadays.

Spices

In Romanian cuisine, there are two
spices that have been largely forgotten
in both sweet and savoury recipes: ginger
and saffron. The first has now come full-
circle to the point where it is considered
new, although there is evidence of it in
16th-century cookery books, and it would
have been used long before that, during
the Roman occupation. Saffron, with its
beautiful colour enhancing noble dishes,
is likely to have disappeared because it
was very expensive, and most certainly
not something for the masses to use during
the last century. They are both now finding
their way back into recipes. In support of
this revival, I used them in a few recipes too.

Caraway seeds are popular in
Transylvanian savoury dishes, but would
have also been used in sweet recipes in
the past. Angelica seeds (wild fennel) have
now disappeared completely, but I took
the liberty of suggesting them as a
flavouring in a few recipes.

In the past, just like today, the use
of ground cinnamon has dominated most
of the other spices, and we are very much
in the habit of sprinkling it on everything.
Nutmeg, cardamom and cloves are still
a long way behind it.

Floral flavours and herbs

We are fond of using fresh herbs in our
cuisine, especially in savoury dishes, which
has given me the opportunity to expand
on this practice and introduce them as
optional ingredients throughout the book.
Flowers and herbs were used centuries ago
to infuse water or syrups, not just as another
flavour but also for a hint of sweetness. Such
was the case with orange blossom and rose
petal waters. In spring, Romanians love
to make elderflower cordial – *socată* – and
I have made a delicate syrup for savarin
cakes with summer berries on page 201.

In many parts of the countryside,
basil was exclusively associated with going
to church on Sundays or other folk beliefs –
people did not use it in cooking, let alone in
a cake. I chose to combine its powerful
aroma with cherries, both at their best
almost in the same season, in my Cherry
and Basil Sour Cream Cake on page 178.

Sage and rosemary usually find
their way into many savoury dishes, but
work equally well in sweet ones too, such
as in Upside-Down Pear and Sage Cake
(page 208) or Toffee Apple and Rosemary
Sauce (page 140). I included tarragon to
infuse honey and drizzle on fruit fritters
(page 159), and mint in an apricot sorbet
(page 229). All of these herbs come together
to describe the flavours of Romania, and
they are perhaps the only time when
I stepped, if only with one foot, outside
of classical recipes.

Magiun and jams

A *magiun* (a very thick fruit jam) is today exclusively associated with plum butter. In the countryside, where often sugar was an expensive ingredient, a *magiun* would not be sweetened, but was cooked slowly and in different stages to extract the natural sweetness of the fruit. Traditionally, it was cooked in large iron kettles, whose lids were sealed with clay, hanging over open fires. When the boiling was over, the *magiun* would be transferred to earthenware pots, and placed in a bread oven after the baking of loaves had finished, when the temperature was low. The aim was to get the top layer of the jam so dry that it would seal the contents underneath. Radu Anton Roman, a much-loved Romanian food ethnographer, has noted that people would also add a thin layer of fat on top, to make sure the jars were properly capped.

Although usually associated with plums, I found a recipe for grape *magiun*, and one for apricot and greengages. In fact, any fruit – even mixed – can be cooked in this way. Many recipes in this book use *magiun*. If you can't buy it, I suggested a method to prepare it in minutes on page 175 – it's not traditional but has a similar result.

Jams, whether raspberry, apricot, summer berry, elder and so on, are used extensively in Eastern European baking. A thousand recipes contain the phrase 'spread some jam' on almost every biscuit or layer of cake. When it didn't affect the recipe, I sometimes used stewed fruit, but you can certainly use your favourite homemade jam or buy one.

Smântână and *brânză de vaci*

Fermented dairy is our magic ingredient in Eastern European baking, especially in Romania. In a country where cattle and sheep are grazing freely on the rich pastures of the Carpathian mountains, dairy foods (including *smântână*, which is similar to crème fraîche; yoghurt; *caimac* or clotted cream) are part of everyday cooking. A spoonful takes your recipe to the next level – creating moreish, soft, melt-in-the-mouth textures that have the right structure to hold fruits, jams or walnut fillings. Even the famous German shredded pancakes – *șmoră* – are made in Banat with yoghurt or crème fraîche.

Another example is *brânză de vaci*, a curd cheese with a crumbly texture that is not moist or liquid. Most of the time, it can be replaced with ricotta mixed, in some cases, with semolina, or you can choose to buy Polish *twaróg*, or German *Topfen*. Cottage cheese is too runny and would need draining in a sieve. You can, of course, make it at home too.

Mere

Apples represent one of the most beloved pie and cake fillings in Romanian baking, offering a tangy, dairy-free alternative to curd cheese. In the autumn, apples are so abundant that you find them sold from roadside stands. Among them, old Romanian apple varieties, such as Batoș, Voinești or Crețesc.

Rom

A lot of Romanian baking recipes contain rum, especially rum essence, which I don't use in any of the recipes in this book. Real rum, white or dark, is a dream, and not only adds its own flavour but also enhances the other ingredients. We have inherited this trick from German baking, where liqueur and brandy are generously used in their recipes. We add it to doughs, syrups and fillings, and there is nothing quite like it in a chocolate ganache or cheesecake. In a few recipes I also use Kirsch, since Romania is a country of cherries and sour cherries, and we are familiar with these flavours. Maraschino is a good alternative too.

Nuci

Walnut trees feel very much at home in Romania's climate, and often grow wild along the streets in the cities, alongside country roads or in people's gardens. The nuts are just as important in our cuisine as almonds and pistachios are to Mediterranean cooking. We grind them to replace flour, or chop to add to cake fillings and for decoration; we toast them with a pinch of salt to stir into chocolate ganache, or simmer with noodles and mix into puddings. They also have religious significance, being associated with fertility and life giving, therefore many festive recipes feature walnuts in combination with dried fruit and wheat – the holy trinity of sacred ingredients in Romania.

A note on technique

Every recipe in this book is easy to make, even though some need two or three stages to complete. It only means that you need to have a little patience sometimes, as opposed to needing to know specialist techniques. There is really nothing in this book that is out of the ordinary for someone who already bakes in their own kitchen.

Chapter 1

Biscuits and Cookies

Step inside any pastry shop in Romania and you will see in the glass cabinet, on the top shelf, an array of cookies called *fursecuri* and *pișcoturi*, which can be bought as an assortment and paid for by weight. These 'petit fours sec' and 'biscotti', since this is the meaning of each respectively, reveal their provenance in our culinary repertoire by their names. The first is French for 'little cookies dried in the oven' and they were a fashionable treat from when Romanians turned Francophiles in the 19th century, and the new generation, educated in Paris, brought home their tastes for refined cuisine. The latter speaks of the Italian influence, when Italians came to work and trade in Romania, bringing their family recipes with them. The biscotti we know today, *pișcoturi*, are ladyfingers, sponge fingers from the Savoy region in the Italian Alps, and not the snappy biscuits cooked twice that you may be familiar with.

Other recipes for cookies in Romania are shortbreads, buttery spritz cookies or light *langue de chat* sandwiched with chocolate ganache or dipped in chocolate glaze, while some are made with ground walnuts and egg whites. These cookies used to be served at fashionable afternoon teas that became popular between the end of the 19th and mid-20th centuries in Romanian towns and cities. We don't associate them exclusively with Christmas, as in Germany, but rather with visits and parties, when we will take an assortment to offer to the host together with a bouquet of flowers.

In addition, we have the traditional *cornulețe*, crescent rolls filled with jam, Turkish delight or walnuts, for which the recipes can vary from yeasted to short doughs. These are the kind of cookies that we make a lot of, so we can share with the neighbours too.

I have selected a few other recipes that belong to different communities around the country, such as Armenian *kurabia* and Swabian almond cookies, as proof of the rich variety of home baking in Romania. With honey being so valued even from ancient times, I also wanted to reveal something almost forgotten in our cookery repertoire: the long tradition of making gingerbread, called *pogacea cu miere*, kept alive by a handful of bakers. It is still made in Transylvania by the Székely people and you can find the story on pages 38-42 along with a recipe.

Biscuits and Cookies

Cookies Studded with Golden Raisins

Fursecuri cu stafide

These cookies are usually part of what I call my 'party platter', alongside *Pricomigdale* (page 33), *Paleuri* (page 30) and *Pișcoturi* (page 32). Easy to make, they are quite thin because they spread during baking, while the texture and a burst of flavour is brought by the chunky golden raisins (or sultanas).

Makes about 20

100 g (3½ oz) unsalted
 butter, softened
70 g (2½ oz/scant ⅓ cup)
 golden caster
 (superfine) sugar
2 medium egg whites
100 g (3½ oz/generous ¾ cup)
 plain (all-purpose) flour
1 teaspoon vanilla extract
2 teaspoons rum
80 g (3 oz/⅔ cup) golden
 raisins (sultanas), whole
1 teaspoon lemon zest

In a mixing bowl, cream the butter to a soft consistency, then add the sugar and beat together until fluffy. Add the egg whites in two batches, incorporating well after each addition. It may look split, but don't worry. Add the flour, vanilla and rum and beat until creamy. Finally, mix in the golden raisins and lemon zest. Cover the bowl and place in the refrigerator for 2 hours until the mixture looks like cold butter.

Meanwhile, preheat the oven to 150°C (non-fan)/300°F/gas 1. Line a baking sheet with baking paper.

Place heaped teaspoonfuls of the mixture on the lined baking sheet, trying to give them a round shape. Bake for 15–18 minutes until a golden ring forms around the edges.

Transfer to a wire rack to cool before serving.

Rum Chocolate Cream Sandwich Cookies

Paleuri

A nostalgic treat, especially for Romanians who live abroad, these cookies are made of delicate *langue de chat*-style biscuits sandwiched together with a dark chocolate ganache. During the Communist regime, they were one of the very few types of cookies that we could still buy in stores. *Paleuri* became a touch of luxury, although eventually even they were ruined by the system's faults, through the use of inferior substitute ingredients. This is a recipe that hopefully restores their true flavour and culinary dignity.

Makes 18

100 g (3½ oz) unsalted butter, softened
100 g (3½ oz/scant ½ cup) golden caster (superfine) sugar
2 medium eggs
120 g (4 oz/1 cup) plain (all-purpose) flour
1 teaspoon vanilla extract
2 teaspoons dark rum

For the filling

75 g (2½ oz) dark chocolate, finely chopped
150 ml (5 fl oz/scant ⅔ cup) double (heavy) cream
5 teaspoons dark rum

For the drizzle

30 g (1 oz) dark chocolate

Preheat the oven to 170°C (non-fan)/340°F/gas 3. Line a large baking sheet (or two) with baking paper.

In a mixing bowl, cream the butter with the sugar until soft, then add the eggs one by one, incorporating well after each addition. Mix in the flour, vanilla and rum and beat until creamy.

Transfer the batter to a piping bag fitted with a 1-cm (½-in) nozzle, and pipe 36 circles, each about 3 cm (1¼ in) in diameter, on the lined baking sheet(s), keeping the nozzle vertical and without swirling. Dip a finger in cold water and tuck in any peaks that stick out.

Bake for 12–14 minutes until the edges turn a deep golden colour and the tops are lightly coloured. Allow to cool on a wire rack.

Meanwhile, make the filling. Place the chocolate in a large bowl. Heat the cream in a small pan, then pour it over the chocolate. Allow to melt together for 1–2 minutes, then slowly mix to a smooth consistency, adding the rum towards the end. Cover the bowl and place it in the refrigerator until firm but not solid.

When you are ready to fill the cookies, briefly whisk the chocolate cream filling to soft peaks. Pipe or use a teaspoon to sandwich two cookies together with a little of the filling. Repeat until you have 18 sandwich cookies, placing them close together on a wire rack or baking tray.

To decorate, melt the dark chocolate for the drizzle. Using a piping bag fitted with a fine nozzle or just a small teaspoon, drizzle the chocolate over all the cookies at once, first going diagonally in one direction, then in the opposite direction to form a criss-cross pattern.

Vanilla Lady Fingers

Pișcoturi cu vanilie

The Romanian name for these cookies comes from 'biscotti', even though these lady fingers don't need to be baked twice. The texture has to be soft and airy on the inside, and firm on the outside, but not quite as crisp as the store-bought ones. At home, we often serve them alongside a glass of Champagne or fizz, as they are associated with dinner parties, New Year's Eve and other special occasions.

Makes 18

2 medium eggs, separated
50 g (2 oz/¼ cup) golden
    caster (superfine) sugar
2 teaspoons vanilla bean paste
60 g (2¼ oz/½ cup) plain
    (all-purpose) flour
½ teaspoon cornflour
    (cornstarch)
40 g (1½ oz/⅓ cup) icing
    (confectioner's) sugar,
    for dusting

Preheat the oven to 170°C (non-fan)/340°F/gas 3. Line a large baking sheet with baking paper or use greased sponge finger trays (pans).

In a mixing bowl, whisk the egg whites to soft peaks, then add 30 g (1¼ oz/2½ tablespoons) of the sugar and whisk until the peaks hold their shape.

In a separate bowl, beat the egg yolks with 20 g (¾ oz/1½ tablespoons) of the sugar and the vanilla paste, then sift the flour with the cornflour over the mixture and mix well. Gently fold in the egg whites.

Transfer the batter to a piping bag fitted with a 1 cm (½ in) plain nozzle and pipe 8 cm (3 in) long 'fingers' onto the lined baking sheet or into the holes of the sponge finger tray. You will need to pipe twice, once from top to bottom, then back up. Dust them with icing sugar and bake for 10 minutes.

Allow to cool on a wire rack before serving.

Walnut and Coffee Macarons

Pricomigdale cu nucă și cafea

These cookies are a kind of macarons made with walnuts instead of almonds. They are served at parties or special occasions, and satisfy even the sweetest tooth, being the perfect companion to a strong black coffee. In this recipe, I added extra chopped walnuts to the mixture, which I have found to improve their texture and nutty flavour. The macarons are soft and gooey, and are a favourite in my family.

Makes 12–14

100 g (3½ oz/generous ¾ cup) walnuts: 60 g (2 oz/½ cup) whole; 40 g (1½ oz/⅓ cup) roughly chopped

50 g (2 oz/generous ¼ cup) soft dark brown sugar

50 g (2 oz/generous ⅓ cup) icing (confectioner's) sugar

40 g (1½ oz/generous ⅓ cup) ground almonds

10 g (5 teaspoons) cornflour (cornstarch)

½ teaspoon instant coffee powder

1 medium egg white

½ teaspoon almond extract

1 tablespoon freshly squeezed lemon juice

Preheat the oven to 170°C (non-fan)/340°F/gas 3. Line a large baking sheet with baking paper.

In a food processor, blitz together the whole walnuts, both types of sugar, the ground almonds, cornflour and instant coffee to a fine texture.

In a separate bowl, gently beat the egg white with the almond extract and lemon juice, then add it to the dry ingredients, blitzing to a paste. Stir in the chopped walnuts.

Using a teaspoon, place generous quantities of the mixture onto the lined baking sheet, leaving 2–3 cm (1 in) between them to allow for spreading.

Bake for 15 minutes.

Remove from the oven and let them cool on the baking sheet. When cool, very gently slide the tip of a sharp knife underneath to help release them from the baking paper.

Serve with a strong coffee.

Rose-Petal Jam Crescents

Cornulețe cu dulceață de trandafiri

We are very fond of these little crescents in Romania and often make more than we need, so that we can take them to neighbours, family and friends. Each family has its own favourite recipe, making the dough either with yeast or baking powder, with added butter or oil, or using *borș*, a fermented wheat juice. The most popular fillings are jam, Turkish delight or walnuts. In this recipe I'm using rose-petal jam, which is exquisite and fragrant, and happens to have the scent of Turkish delight. The crescents are so delicate that they melt in the mouth right away.

Makes about 16

250 g (9 oz/2 cups) plain (all-purpose) flour, plus extra for dusting
125 g (4 oz) unsalted butter
20 g (¾ oz/2 tablespoons) golden caster (superfine) sugar
1 medium egg yolk
75 g (2½ oz/⅓ cup) sour cream
1 tablespoon rosewater
1 teaspoon baking powder
icing (confectioner's) sugar, for dusting

For the filling

150 g (5 oz/½ cup) Rose-Petal Confiture (page 262 or store-bought), mixed with 1 teaspoon lemon juice
or
9 pieces of rose-flavoured Turkish delight, diced

Alternative filling

prune filling on page 110

In a mixing bowl, rub the flour and butter together until they resemble breadcrumbs. Add the sugar, egg yolk, sour cream, rosewater and baking powder, and mix until a dough forms. Transfer it to a piece of clingfilm (plastic wrap) and bring the dough together by hand without kneading much. Cover and refrigerate for 1 hour.

Preheat the oven to 180°C (non-fan)/350°F/gas 4. Line a baking sheet with baking paper. Lightly flour your work surface.

Divide the pastry dough in half. Keep one half in the refrigerator while you roll out the other to a circle, at least 24 cm (9½ in) in diameter. Place a plate of that size on top of the pastry and trim neatly around the edges. Divide the circle into quarters, then cut each quarter in half again to achieve 8 wedges of pastry. Place 1 teaspoonful of jam (or a few pieces of Turkish delight) at the wider end of each wedge and roll up. Press to seal the edges and place on the baking sheet.

Repeat with the second half of the pastry dough.

Bake for 15–18 minutes on a lower shelf until lightly golden and just firm enough to the touch for you to be able to lift them quickly onto a cooling rack. They will firm up as they cool.

Serve slightly warm, dusted with icing sugar.

Raspberry and Chocolate Walnut Cookies

Işlere or Bad Ischler cookies

Işlere have a glorious history, being one of the favourite cookies of the Austrian Emperor Franz Joseph when on holiday in his beloved spa town, Bad Ischl. From here, they started their journey through Eastern Europe, being wholeheartedly adopted and adapted by home bakers throughout the Habsburg Empire. Today, they are also the culinary emblem of Brașov, one of the most important historic Saxon cities in Transylvania. They are made with walnuts rather than almonds, and filled with either chocolate cream or raspberry jam, which is my favourite. Most versions are completely glazed in chocolate, which can get a bit messy, therefore it is perfectly acceptable if you only spread the glaze on top.

Makes 10

50 g (2 oz/generous ⅓ cup) blanched hazelnuts
50 g (2 oz/½ cup) walnut halves
160 g (5½ oz/1¼ cups) plain (all-purpose) flour
100 g (3½ oz) unsalted butter, diced
50 g (2 oz/¼ cup) caster (superfine) sugar
1 teaspoon lemon zest

For the filling

150 g (5 oz/½ cup) seedless raspberry conserve

For the glaze

150 g (5 oz) dark chocolate

Preheat the oven to 180°C (non-fan)/350°F/gas 4.

Spread the blanched hazelnuts over a baking sheet and roast them in the oven for 10 minutes, then remove and let cool.

In a food processor, blitz together the hazelnuts and walnuts until they turn into a fine meal. Add the flour and butter and process until the mixture resembles rough breadcrumbs. Add the sugar and lemon zest and pulse again 4–5 times until it starts to form a dough.

Tip the dough onto a work surface and bring it together quickly using your fingertips, pressing and turning, trying not to knead. Divide in half, then cover and refrigerate for 1 hour.

Roll out one half of the dough between two large pieces of baking paper to a 4 mm (¼ in) thickness. Using a 6 cm (2½ in) pastry cutter, cut out 10 discs and place them on a lined baking sheet. Repeat with the other half of the dough until you have 20 discs, then place them in the refrigerator for 1 hour.

Meanwhile, preheat the oven to 170°C (non-fan)/340°F/gas 3.

Bake the cookies for 10–12 minutes until slightly golden.

Allow to cool on the baking sheet for 5 minutes, then use a palette knife to transfer the cookies to a wire cooling rack.

When completely cool, sandwich the cookies with 1 teaspoonful of raspberry conserve in the middle.

Make the glaze by melting the chocolate in a bowl placed over a pan of simmering water (ensuring the base of the bowl does not touch the water) or microwave to a liquid consistency. While still warm, spoon a little of the glaze over the top of each cookie, or cover it completely. Allow to set before serving.

Transylvanian Székelys
Secuii din Transilvania

✕ ✕ ✕ ✕ ✕ ✕ ✕ ✕ ✕ ✕ ✕ ✕ ✕ ✕ ✕ ✕ ✕ ✕

Terra Siculorum

The Székely live in one of the most spectacular regions in Transylvania, a patchwork of forests and valleys, punctuated by healing waters and Carpathian mountain peaks. A land paved with legends and artistic spirit, it is known as Ținutul Secuiesc, *Szekelyfold*, or *Terra Siculorum* in Latin. Its people are single-minded, independent thinkers and fiercely proud of their culture and history.

One of the warrior elites of Central Asian nomadic tribes, Székely first settled in today's western Hungary, and from there travelled east to Transylvania. With their remarkable military skills, they helped the Arpadian Magyar dynasty to establish their rule over these lands, and the kings of Hungary to influence the medieval structures of Europe. In fact, Saint Margaret of Scotland is believed to have been the niece of the first Hungarian king, St Stephen I. Centuries later, landowners in the Székely region, educated at European universities and forming the elite of the Habsburg administration, had connections with European royal families. Prince Charles, the current heir to the British throne, discovered that his great-great-grandmother Klaudia Rhédey used to live in the town of Sângeorgiu de Pădure in Transylvania.

Székely land was organised as a federation of seats, with the right to have their own laws and some fiscal freedom, and it remained more or less the same for over six hundred years. With their war skills and defence power at the feet of the Carpathian mountains, Székely fought to protect Europe from the nomadic tribes and the over-expanding Ottoman Empire.

In the 15th century, their military elites, all free men, were invited to join the Union of Three Nations and rule Transylvania alongside the politically powerful Magyars and commercially influential Saxons. The term 'nation' referred to status rather than ethnicity: noblemen, merchants and military. In the same region also lived Romanians, Magyar and Saxon peasantry, who were not all free and had no political representation, with Romanians making up the bulk of the serf population.

This is when a seed was sown. The revolutions that swept through Europe in 1848 found Székely seats being the first to abolish serfdom in Transylvania. Balázs Orbán, a visionary Székely nobleman, talked about the right of Romanians to speak their own language and practice their own religion. Little did he know that this future was to be forged in 1918, when Transylvania joined Romania after the end of the Austro-Hungarian Empire, creating the state we know today.

The book of legends

The last 100 years were possibly the most controversial and convoluted in Székely history, as they were for the whole Romanian nation. A revival movement is gathering momentum, rediscovering old traditions and artisan skills, and educating the new generations in folk art and Székely history.

Szabolcs Fazakas is the founder of Legendarium, an animation studio with Hollywood credentials, which turns Székely folk legends into cartoon films. He says: 'We have the most beautiful folk stories to tell. The characters are very sweet, always well intended and doing a good deed, whether fixing someone's damaged roof, or helping an old lady with the work in the field.' In watching their films, I realise how many community values are in these legends: look after your neighbours, work towards a greater good and respect each other. They are rather like Scouting manuals with the magical intervention of rivers and forests, although strikingly based on the realities of life. In the films you encounter the Tatar invaders, the King of Hungary, the village priest, and all are quite real. Perhaps the first historical fictions of their time, these legends are brilliant pieces of storytelling about how Székely people see themselves.

Székely honey *pogacea*

The artistic flair of the Székely defines who they are, and one particular skill has lasted since medieval times: the making of Székely honey *pogacea*, or gingerbread.

'Its velvety softness was given by the mixture of honey and rye, and there was so much flavour. A gingerbread maker had to become a real sculptor and develop a sense of proportion, space and of the beautiful.' So wrote Károly Tar in his book *Transylvanian Honey Bread* in 1994. Gingerbread had been part of the Székely identity for centuries. Known as honey bread, it was unmissable on market days or at religious fairs.

The Transylvanian apiaries were so famous for their honey that in 1370, the King of Hungary granted duty-free privileges to the Saxon-Germans of Sibiu, who traded in wax with Vienna, Bohemia and Venice. It set an auspicious basis for the Székely taking up gingerbread-making (and the production of mead!), using good-quality honey and the excellent flour that the Transylvanian mills were producing. For this reason, most of the baking utensils and techniques of the process were known by German names.

The spicy bread was originally served with meat dishes, before it became confined to market fairs as a material for religious tokens, edible gifts and souvenirs. *Pogacea* is a Slavic name, as that used to be the lingua franca of the region – a generic word for flat barley breads, quite possibly the predecessors of leavened bread. The Székelyland climate was ideal for cultivating rye, which in time became the signature ingredient in their gingerbread recipes.

A price regulation regarding gingerbread-making, issued by the Hungarian royal court in the 15th century, listed the following ingredients: saffron, ginger, cinnamon, ground pepper, cloves, angelica seeds, nutmeg, raisins and even chestnuts from Italy. Honey was listed alongside cane sugar and 'wood oil', meaning olive oil.

The craft of making gingerbread in Transylvania was initially part of either the beekeepers', millers' or bakers' Guilds and only later did it start to be organised into a distinct profession, especially in towns. In Székely villages, the craft was practised in private homes and was not recognised by a Guild – it was a way for the women to top up their incomes.

The oldest technique was to press the dough into carved wooden moulds, which each baker had to carve with a unique design. Initially, the designs were puppets, which people believed to have healing powers. In the Székely villages, most of these moulds were round, and the favourite patterns were motifs of folk art, such as tulips and flowers, and intricate

designs depicting folk costumes or the hussars' military uniforms.

Târgu Secuiesc was the oldest market town of gingerbread-making in the Székely region. Every autumn, the craftsmen would make a journey by cart to the neighbouring villages to purchase the honey. They would buy whole honeycombs, extract the honey to sell separately, then wash the combs with water. This mixture was later warmed and used to make the gingerbread. The rest of the empty comb would be pressed into blocks and sold to candlemakers.

At the beginning of the 20th century, a new technique was to cut out the gingerbread cookies into different shapes, glaze them with icing (confectioner's) sugar and elaborately decorate in different colours. These have endured the test of time, possibly because the customers loved the bright, eye-catching myriad colours. The market fairs throughout Transylvania were filled with gingerbread stalls, to the delight of audiences of all ages. Girls and young ladies preferred cookies cut into doll and heart shapes, or ladybirds, fruit baskets and religious scenes. Boys apparently loved the hussar-shaped cookies, those soldiers whose bravery and moustaches were legendary.

Károly Tar talked about the creativity at the beginning of the 20th century as being 'like a shoreless river in which ideas floated to their liking'. After World War II, many artisans were deported to labour camps in Russia, and on their return the lack of basic ingredients made it impossible to bake gingerbread. So, they applied for jobs in factories and paper mills, abandoning the traditional skills of their families.

Today, opinions are divided over whether the artisans should return to the old technique of making traditional moulded gingerbread or whether they should just satisfy a market that wants colourful, flowery, cut-out cookies, often iced in their favourite Disney characters. The responsibility lies equally on the makers' as well as on the customers' shoulders.

Biscuits and Cookies

Székely Soft Honey Gingerbread

Pogacea secuiască cu miere

× × × × × × × × × × × × × × × × × × × ×

This Székely gingerbread is glazed in intense colours to offer a contrasting base for the decorations on top. In the past, these colours were extracted from fruits, plants or insects: cochineal dye for red, spinach for green and saffron for yellow. I bought the ones in the photo from a local artisan in Târgu Secuiesc, who makes these beautiful tulip-shaped cookies. I don't glaze my gingerbread, but have offered an alternative suggestion for how to decorate. If you wish, you can use a cookie stamp instead of decorating, or serve them plain, just cut into shapes.

You will need to start making these a day in advance.

Makes 18–20

150 ml (5 fl oz/scant ⅔ cup) honey
35 ml (2 tablespoons plus 1 teaspoon) water
25 g (¾ oz) unsalted butter
1 medium egg yolk
70 g (2½ oz/¾ cup) rye flour
150 g (5 oz/1¼ cups) plain (all-purpose) flour, plus extra for dusting
1 teaspoon baking powder
1 teaspoon ground cinnamon
¼ teaspoon ground cardamom
½ teaspoon ground nutmeg
¼ teaspoon ground cloves
3 teaspoons ground ginger
finely grated zest of 2 oranges

To decorate (optional)

1 large egg white
250 g (9 oz/2 cups) icing (confectioner's) sugar
1 teaspoon liquid glucose
red, green or yellow food colouring gels

Put the honey, water and butter in a small saucepan and bring almost to a simmer, allowing the butter to melt. Allow to cool, then stir in the egg yolk.

In a mixing bowl, mix together the flours with the baking powder, spices and orange zest, then pour over the honey mixture. Mix well to form a paste, cover the bowl and place in the refrigerator overnight.

The following day, preheat the oven to 180°C (non-fan)/350°F/gas 4. Line a baking sheet with baking paper.

Knead the dough briefly, then turn out onto a floured work surface and roll the dough out to a 6 mm (¼ in) thickness. Use a 7 cm (3 in) diameter cookie cutter (or a shape of your choice) to cut the gingerbread shapes out, and place them on the baking sheet.

Bake for 10-12 minutes.

Allow to cool completely on a wire rack.

To decorate, first whisk the egg white to soft peaks, then add the sugar gradually and the liquid glucose at the end, whisking to combine. Add the colour gel a little at a time, until you have the desired shade. First, make the red base and brush the cookies with it in a thin layer. Allow to dry for a few hours before you make more royal icing in your desired colours and pipe as you wish.

Swabian Almond Cookies

Fursecuri şvăbeşti cu migdale

These cookies are made by the German Swabians in the Banat region of western Romania. Almond paste and marzipan are the unmistakable symbols of German baking. I was told that the cookies used to be offered as wedding favours, since their petite size was ideal for gifts.

Makes 14

150 g (5 oz/1½ cups) ground almonds
50 g (2 oz/¼ cup) golden caster (superfine) sugar
20 g (¾ oz/3 tablespoons) icing (confectioner's) sugar
1 medium egg
30 g (1 oz/¼ cup) plain (all-purpose) flour
1 teaspoon almond extract
42 blanched almonds

For the glaze

1 egg yolk mixed with 1 tablespoon water

In a food processor, pulse together the ground almonds with the sugars and egg to a paste consistency. Add the flour and almond extract and combine well. Place in the refrigerator for 1 hour.

Preheat the oven to 160°C (non-fan)/320°F/gas 2. Line a baking sheet with baking paper.

Form the dough into 8 g (¼ oz) balls and place on the lined baking sheet. Stud each cookie ball with 3 almonds, pressing them into the top of the dough in the shape of a flower. Brush each cookie with the glaze.

Bake for 12–15 minutes on a lower shelf until they start to turn golden.

Allow to cool completely on the baking sheet, then slide a sharp knife underneath each to release from the baking paper. Enjoy.

Cocoa and Vanilla Cookies

Fursecuri în două culori

I chose to include these cookies because they are fun to make and have two flavours in one. The patterns and shapes can vary almost to a form of art, according to one's patience and skill. The recipe below makes one of the easiest patterns and is a good starting point for you to test the waters. They are of German influence in our cuisine and especially popular at Christmas time.

Makes about 28

250 g (9 oz/2 cups) plain (all-purpose) flour, plus extra for dusting
135 g (4½ oz) unsalted butter, cold and diced
70 g (2½ oz/generous ½ cup) icing (confectioner's) sugar
1 medium egg
1 tablespoon water
1 teaspoon vanilla paste
8 g (¼ oz/1 tablespoon) cocoa powder
1 pinch of ground cardamom

For the glaze

1 egg yolk mixed with 1 tablespoon water

In a food processor, mix together the flour and butter until they resemble breadcrumbs. Add the sugar, egg, water and vanilla, pulsing a few times until a dough forms.

Divide the dough into two equal parts and return one half to the food processor. Add the cocoa powder and cardamom, and mix together briefly. Turn the dough out onto a piece of clingfilm (plastic wrap) and form it into a ball by bringing the dough together with the palm of your hands and fingertips. Flatten it, wrap and place in the refrigerator.

Use the same method to bring the other half of the dough together, wrap and place in the refrigerator for 10 minutes, or until firm enough to roll while still being flexible.

Roll both halves out to a rectangular shape of the same size and thickness, roughly 20 x 25 cm (8 x 10 in) and 4 mm (just under ¼ in) thick. Trim the edges if necessary. You can flour your work surface lightly if it gets too sticky. Brush the vanilla rectangle with some of the egg yolk glaze, then place the cocoa rectangle on top. Roll both layers up together like a huge cigar, then gently press and roll a few times to ensure that both layers are sticking together. Wrap and place in the refrigerator for 1 hour.

Preheat the oven to 180°C (non-fan)/350°F/gas 4. Line a baking sheet with baking paper.

Unwrap the dough and cut the log into 6 mm (just over ¼ in) slices, placing them flat on the lined baking sheet.

Bake for 15 minutes, or until they start to change colour slightly around the edges.

Allow to cool and enjoy.

Fennel and Aniseed Shortbreads

Biscuiți cu anason și fenicul

Aniseed used to be a popular spice in Romanian recipes up until the middle of the 20th century, when it suddenly vanished completely, possibly because it was hard to find. I came across it in a couple of old recipes for cookies and bread puddings, used alongside angelica seeds, which is wild fennel. Together, both spices enhance each other's warm aromas, and pair well with the sweetness of the shortbread.

Makes 20

150 g (5 oz) unsalted butter, cold and diced
250 g (9 oz/2 cups) plain (all-purpose) flour, plus extra for dusting
60 g (2¼ oz/¼ cup) caster (superfine) sugar
1 medium egg
½ teaspoon baking powder
1 teaspoon lemon zest
2 tablespoons white wine or water
2 teaspoons crushed fennel seeds
2 teaspoons crushed aniseeds or ground aniseed

To decorate

2 teaspoons aniseeds

In a mixing bowl, use your fingertips to rub the butter into the flour until crumbly, or you can use a food processor and pulse a few times. Add the rest of the ingredients and mix with a fork until the dough sticks together. Press into a rectangle, wrap in clingfilm (plastic wrap) and chill in the refrigerator for 40 minutes.

Line a baking sheet with baking paper.

Flour your work surface and the top of the pastry and roll it out to a rectangle, 8 mm (⅓ in) thick, trimming the edges to make them neat. Cut into 5 cm (2 in) square biscuits. Use a tiny cookie cutter to cut out shapes in the middle, then sprinkle the aniseeds on top to decorate. Gather all the trimmings and roll again (if they are too soft to roll, chill for a few more minutes) until you have used up all the dough. Place the biscuits on the lined baking sheet and chill in the refrigerator for a further 30 minutes.

Meanwhile, preheat the oven to 180°C (non-fan)/350°F/gas 4.

Bake the cookies for 12–15 minutes until lightly golden.

Allow to cool on the baking sheet for a few minutes, then transfer to a wire cooling rack to cool completely.

Armenian Kurabia Shortbread with Mahlep

Corăbioare armeneşti

These iconic Armenian shortbreads are usually served on large trays at weddings and celebrations. Talking to Armenians in Romania, I noticed that almost every gathering is a reason to celebrate, usually with *kurabia*, *pakhlava*, herbal tea and coffee. I used mahlep in this recipe for its delicate cherry fragrance at the recommendation of Paul Agopian, who writes about the Armenian community in Romania. *Kurabia* is traditionally made into the shape of the sun, which was venerated in pre-Christian times, and it has kept this archaic spherical shape ever since.

Makes 15

120 g (4 oz) unsalted butter, softened but not melted
60 g (2¼ oz/¼ cup) golden caster (superfine) sugar
180 g (6½ oz/1½ cups) plain (all-purpose) flour
10 g (½ oz/1 tablespoon) mahlep (mahleb), plus extra for decorating
icing (confectioner's) sugar, for rolling

Line a large baking sheet with baking paper.

In a mixing bowl, cream the butter with the sugar until fluffy, then add the flour and mahlep. Mix briefly, then bring the dough together by hand, kneading it 2–3 times. Tear the dough into 25 g (just under 1 oz) balls, place them on the lined baking tray and gently press on the tops to flatten them slightly. Cover and refrigerate for 2 hours. If you can, place the tray in the freezer for a further 10 minutes.

Preheat the oven to 180°C (non-fan)/350°F/gas 4.

Bake for 15 minutes on a lower shelf. Keep an eye on them as they don't need to change colour.

Allow to cool on a wire rack, then roll in icing sugar. Use the tiniest pinch of mahlep to sprinkle on top of each cookie, but be careful since too much of it can turn the flavours bitter.

Chapter 2
Pies

In the varied Romanian baking repertoire, *plăcinte* are the most famous pies of all. They usually have only two layers of dough, one at the base and one on top, and they don't meet to cover the sides. Baked in large trays and cut into rectangular or square slices, they are served cold, stacked on top of each other on a plate and left on the table for everyone to snack on. While the most popular sweet fillings are either apple or curd cheese, there is a seasonal one in the autumn with pumpkin, which is just as loved. The pies need a fruit or veg that can stay relatively firm when baked, rather than become too soft.

The origin of *plăcinte* goes back to ancient Greece and the Roman Empire, where skilful bakers used to make *plakous* or *placentae*, flatbreads filled with honey and cheese. Long before the Roman conquest of some parts of today's Romania, the Greeks established trade settlements at the mouth of the Danube and along the Black Sea coast, to facilitate commerce with the neighbouring tribes. It is possible that along these trading routes they brought with them the method of making pies, which remained in our repetoire ever since.

A good example of how popular they were can be found in an intriguing story from the 18th century, written by the Italian secretary of Prince Brâncoveanu in the southern principality of Wallachia. Anton-Maria Del Chiaro described the royal custom of serving a *plăcintă cu răvaşe* at the end of a dinner, a huge pie containing among the filling different words written on small pieces of paper or fabric. 'Pride', 'greed', 'envy' and 'power' were amongst the most frequent, and guests had no choice but to read them out loud amid the laughter of the others who would wittily add their own comments.

The traditional *plăcintă* dough was made only with flour and water, however it's rarely used today. Called *aluat* in Romanian, it now also contains eggs, dairy and butter or oil, the layers being rolled rather than pulled as in filo. Traditionally, it should not be leavened, but more often than not recipes do use yeast, in which case the pie has a bread-like texture, while others use bicarbonate of soda (baking soda) or baking powder, adding more softness. Since I already mentioned filo, I have to add, without wishing to confuse matters, that we call it *foi de plăcintă* ('pie leaves') and it can sometimes replace the rolled layers, in which case we use more than two.

Plăcinte today have as many regional variations as individual ones, bakers adding their own preferences. I have selected those recipes that can give you an idea of the different types of dough, shapes and fillings, and also different methods. I also tell the inspirational story of the Saxon villages in Transylvania and their iconic pie called *lichiu* (see pages 67–70). I tested all the variations on this pie and settled on the one in this chapter, as it gives you the full spectrum of all its possible flavours.

Apple and Walnut Pie

Plăcintă cu mere

This is one of the most famous pies in Romania. It is not too sweet,
allowing the flavour of the apples to take centre stage.

Serves 8

200 g (7 oz/scant 1 cup)
   clotted cream or *caimac*
100 g (3½ oz/scant ½ cup)
   crème fraîche
15 g (½ oz) unsalted butter,
   softened
50 g (2 oz/¼ cup) caster
   (superfine) sugar
1 teaspoon vanilla bean paste
300 g (10½ oz/2½ cups) plain
   (all-purpose) flour
1 tablespoon cold water
icing (confectioner's) sugar,
   for dusting

For the filling

550–600 g (1 lb 3½ oz–1 lb 5 oz)
   apples (such as Bramley,
   Braeburn, Cox or Granny
   Smith), grated
80 g (3oz/⅓ cup) caster
   (superfine) sugar
juice of 1 lemon
50 g (2 oz/scant ½ cup)
   chopped walnuts
2 teaspoons ground cinnamon

To make the dough, combine the clotted cream, crème fraîche and
butter in a mixing bowl with the sugar and vanilla. Using a fork, mix
in the flour in two batches, add the water, then use your hands to press
and pinch the dough together. It may look at little dry at first, but
transfer it to the work surface and knead lightly into a ball. Even if
it doesn't look too smooth, return it to the bowl, cover with a dish
towel and leave to rest for 30 minutes (in the refrigerator if the
kitchen is hot).

Preheat the oven to 180°C (non-fan)/350°F/gas 4. Grease and line
the base of a non-stick baking tin (pan), 18 x 24 cm (7 x 9½ in)
and at least 6 cm (2¼ in) deep.

To make the filling, place the grated apples in a bowl, sprinkle with
half of the sugar, add the lemon juice and set aside.

Split the ball of dough in half and roll out one half to the shape of the
baking tin. Evenly press the dough into the tin with your fingers, prick
it all over with a fork, then sprinkle the walnuts on top.

Squeeze as much juice as you can from the grated apples, discarding
the liquid. Spread the apples evenly on top of the walnuts, then sprinkle
over the remaining sugar and the ground cinnamon. Roll out the other
half of the dough to the size of the tin and place it on top of the pie
to cover.

Bake on the lower rack of the oven for 45 minutes, covering the top
with kitchen foil if it turns too dark.

Allow to cool in the tin covered with a clean cloth. Cut into slices
while slightly warm, dust with icing sugar and serve.

Moldavian Layered Pie with Hemp Cream

Julfe moldovenești

This pie is endearingly named *Pelincile Domnului*, which means 'swaddling blankets of baby Jesus'. Traditionally made on Christmas Eve in Moldavia, eastern Romania, it represents a custom to gather every 'fruit of the earth' on the table, such as grains and seeds that can sprout in the next season. Hemp was an important crop in the region, so it makes an appearance alongside honey and wheat. The ground seeds make a filling called *julfa*, which can also be used in other dishes as an alternative to soft dairy cheese. The usual number of layers is twelve, but feel free to experiment with fewer layers while practising your technique.

Serves 16

400 g (14 oz/3¼ cups) plain (all-purpose) flour, plus extra for dusting
250 ml (8½ fl oz/1 cup) water
1 pinch of salt

For the filling

250 g (9 oz/2 cups) pumpkin seeds
250 g (9 oz/2 cups) hulled hemp seeds, plus extra to serve (optional)
3 tablespoons honey
125 ml (4 fl oz/½ cup) hemp milk, any non-dairy milk or water

For the syrup

450 ml (15 fl oz/1¾ cups) water
125 g (4 oz/generous ½ cup) golden caster (superfine) sugar
2 tablespoons honey
juice and zest of 1 lemon

Combine the flour, water and salt in a bowl and knead to a firm dough. Leave to rest at room temperature for 15 minutes, then knead again and leave to rest for a further 15 minutes.

Set a large cast-iron (or non-stick) frying pan (skillet) over a medium heat. Don't add any oil.

Divide the dough into 12 pieces, about 50 g (2 oz) each. On a floured work surface, roll and stretch one ball to a circle, 25 cm (10 in) in diameter (or as large as your pan). Keep dusting with a little flour underneath and on top of the dough, so you can roll and stretch it very thinly by hand. Lift and place in the hot pan (don't worry if it loses its shape slightly) and cook for 3 minutes, then flip and cook the other side for a further 3 minutes. It needs to have the texture of a thin, dry biscuit. Repeat with the remaining dough balls, rolling and cooking one at a time. Stack them on a plate or a wire cooling rack.

To make the filling, grind the pumpkin seeds to a powder in a food processor. Add the hemp seeds and blitz together. Add the honey, then gradually add the milk or water, with the motor at medium speed, until the mixture reaches a soft, spreadable consistency. Set aside.

To make the syrup, bring all the ingredients to the boil in a pan, then reduce the heat and simmer for 15 minutes until thickened. Pour into a large shallow dish, wide enough to fit one of the flatbreads inside.

To assemble the pie, soak a flatbread in the syrup for 30 seconds, then place it in a dish or a plate with a deep lip. Spread the flatbread with a thin layer of the filling. Repeat with all the remaining flatbreads, leaving the top one plain. You can spoon a little of the remaining syrup on top. Wrap the dish or plate in clingfilm (plastic wrap), then place a tray on top and weight it down with something heavy. This will ensure that the layers are pressed evenly (don't worry if they crack). Leave for 24 hours, then slice and serve.

You can serve as it is or save a couple of tablespoons of the filling to spread on top and sprinkle with a few hulled hemp seeds.

Curd Cheese and Golden Raisin Pie

Plăcintă cu brânză

This is the second most-famous sweet pie in Romania, gently scented with lemon zest and golden raisins (sultanas). Together with its twin sister the apple pie (page 57), they make an interchangeable duo on Romanian tables. You can swap the fillings easily for a slightly different variation.

Serves 8

350 g (12 oz/2¾ cups) plain (all-purpose) flour
½ teaspoon baking powder
2 medium eggs
1 tablespoon sunflower oil
120 ml (4 fl oz/½ cup) full-fat milk, lukewarm

For the filling

250 g (9 oz/1 generous cup) full-fat curd cheese (Romanian *brânză de vaci* or ricotta)
80 g (3 oz/⅓ cup) crème fraîche
1 large egg
80 g (3oz/⅓ cup) caster (superfine) sugar
100 g (3½ oz/generous ¾ cup) golden raisins (sultanas)
finely grated zest of 1 lemon
40 g (1½ oz/⅓ cup) fine semolina

To finish

2 teaspoons melted butter mixed with 2 teaspoons milk, for brushing
icing (confectioner's) sugar, for dusting

Preheat the oven to 180°C (non-fan)/350°F/gas 4. Grease and line the base of a non-stick baking tin (pan), 18 x 24 cm (7 x 9½ in) and at least 6 cm (2¼ in) deep.

In a mixing bowl, combine the flour with the baking powder. In a separate bowl, whisk together the eggs, oil and milk. Add the wet mixture to the flour, kneading until the dough comes away from the sides of the bowl. Cover and allow to rest at room temperature while you prepare the filling.

To make the filling, mix all the ingredients together in a bowl.

Split the ball of dough in half and roll out one half to the shape of the baking tin. Evenly press the dough into the tin with your fingers, prick it all over with a fork, then bake for 10 minutes.

Remove from the oven and spread the filling on top of the pastry. Roll out the other half of the dough to the size of the tin and place it on top of the pie to cover, tucking in the sides. Brush with the butter mixture.

Bake for 45 minutes, covering the top with kitchen foil if it turns too dark.

Allow to cool in the tin covered with a clean cloth. This pie reaches its ideal consistency after 3 hours of resting, or even the next day. Cut into small slices and dust with icing sugar to serve.

Transylvanian Griddle Breads with Cheese and Honey

Plăcintă ardelenească la tigaie cu urdă și miere

These flatbread-style pies come in many variations throughout Romania and each of them is considered to be key to the cultural identity of the region you eat them in. They are called *plăcinte*, *turte*, *scovergi*, *pite* or *lipii*, and can be fried or grilled. There is a tradition in Ardeal, another name for Transylvania, to cook the pies on a *lespede*, which is a baking stone. A typical sweet filling can either be curd cheese or jam, drizzled with honey or dusted with icing (confectioner's) sugar. I read that in old times these pies were so important that even a young lady's dowry would include one of them. I have chosen to make a recipe with curd cheese, since it is easier to fold and cook, and irresistible when served with honey.

Makes 6

180 g (6½ oz) curd cheese (Romanian *brânză de vaci* or set cottage cheese)
4 tablespoons sunflower oil, for cooking
runny honey, for drizzling

For the dough

300 g (10½ oz/2½ cups) plain (all-purpose) flour, plus extra for dusting
20 g (¾ oz/2 tablespoons) golden caster (superfine) sugar
7 g (1 sachet) fast-action dried yeast
100 ml (3½ fl oz/scant ½ cup) water
5 tablespoons milk
2 tablespoons sunflower oil
1 pinch of salt

If you are using cottage cheese for the filling, drain it of any excess water beforehand.

Make the dough by combining all the ingredients together in a bowl, then knead until soft and silky. Cover and leave to rest at room temperature for 1 hour.

Set a cast-iron or non-stick frying pan (skillet) over a medium–high heat.

Flour your work surface and hands generously, then divide the dough into 6 equal parts. Roll one piece out to a circle, 25–30 cm (10–12 in) in diameter. Crumble (or spread) a sixth of the cheese on top. Bring the sides to the middle in 7 or 8 folds, overlapping them slightly, then press with your hands or gently use a rolling pin to flatten and seal them. Repeat until you have 6 filled breads ready to be cooked.

Oil the hot pan with about 1 tablespoon of oil. Cook each pie on both sides for a few minutes until golden brown. Transfer to a plate and cover with a beeswax wrap or a reusable plastic bag (the steam will keep them soft) while you cook the rest.

Serve warm, drizzled with honey.

Transylvanian Saxons
Sașii din Transilvania

'Anyway, the blue eyes, flaxen hair and Teutonic speech that I met in those arcades and market-places could just as well have belonged a thousand miles to the west. Nobody has ever confused them with later Germanic settlers in re-conquered Hungary – the Arad Swabians, for instance. It seemed a miracle that they and their towns and hamlets and their skills and their language should have weathered the past eight centuries of commotion with so little damage.'

So wrote Patrick Leigh Fermor in his novel *Between the Woods and the Water*, published in 1986. Little did he realise that only three years later, after the fall of the Communist regime in December 1989, tens of thousands of Saxons would leave their villages for Germany, worn out by the political control and incapable of envisaging a future in what had been their homeland for over 800 years. The villages faced mass exodus in the space of one year. Those who decided to stay witnessed the crumbling of ancestral homes, the alteration of the landscape and complete disintegration of communities.

A distinct yet integral part of Romanian culture

Looking around at the empty homes in her own village, where her family had lived for centuries, Caroline Fernolend decided to do something about it. It may have become almost unrecognisable, but Caroline knew how a Saxon village was supposed to work. She applied the ancestral principles first in Viscri, and later to other neighbouring locations, and established what is now known as the Saxon self-sufficient village prototype. Her philosophy: 'If people are proud of their history, of the place they live in, and they can also make a living here, we can all prosper together, respect each other no matter where we come from. With this one project in mind, we solve an economic issue, as well as a social and cultural one.'

Help was at first offered by the Mihai Eminescu Trust, whose headquarters were then in the UK, and by volunteers from all over Europe. Many homes and public buildings were restored in such a way that local people learned new skills and old traditional building methods, using local materials and fabrics. This encouraged collateral businesses to thrive. The bricks, for instance, were bought from the brickmaker in the village, who left his job in Hungary to make his own future at home, and to pass on a craft to his children and grandchildren. Today, all the skills needed for restorations and for running B&Bs or artisan workshops are found within these villages.

'We try to make the money go around locally, so everyone is involved and everyone gains,' says Caroline, who was handed the reins of Mihai Eminescu Trust in Romania and works with a small team of fiercely passionate young people. Even the Romany groups, so villainised in the past for moving illegally into the empty Saxon houses, now have their own jobs and contributions to make. 'Women are weaving woollen socks, or making traditional Saxon felt shoes; men have their own crafts and those who don't, offer cart or horse rides to tourists and visitors.'

This self-reliant village, where there are neither poor nor beggars but only working people, reflects very much the old Saxon way of living.

'The church is my fortress'

Saxons were invited to settle in Transylvania in the early 13th century, to defend the border from the Tatar and later from Ottoman invasions, and to make the area more prosperous. Initially, they came from Magdeburg in Saxony, hence the name, later to be joined by others from different German-speaking regions, including from Flanders in Belgium, Mosel in France and Luxembourg. In exchange, they were given fertile land and permitted to use their own legal system, tax concessions and autonomy. Their powerful status in the cities as part of the Union of Three Nations governing Transylvania, allowed them to create a flourishing network of villages and market towns, to establish trade routes from the Black Sea to Western and Northern Europe, and to dominate the commerce between Transylvania and the two Romanian principalities. This was the engine of the Saxon towns.

In the countryside, at the heart of a Saxon community, stood the church fortress. An imposing building surrounded by double walls and protected by towers, which in times of war could have provided shelter for everyone in the village. Through centuries, when the Tatars and Ottomans attacked with regularity, these churches represented the physical and religious survival of the Saxons: 'The LORD is my rock, my fortress, and the One who rescues me.' (*Psalm 18*)

The towers were used for food storage, and in times of peace as a village store, where each family was allowed twice a week to draw provisions from their own stores. The Lardo Tower would have been for storing ham, lardo and charcuterie; the Prune Tower for prunes and other dried fruit. Each family had their own particular stamp, used to mark the lardo after slicing or the provision bags after they had been opened.

Lichiu

Transylvanian Saxon cuisine has been governed by practicality, using ingredients that were produced in the household or village. It is an ingenious cuisine, and we can find fruit sauces served with meat, or dried fruits added to soups. When it comes to desserts, the line is blurred again, because sometimes they are lunch too, like the *papanași* on page 136 or *lichiu* on page 70.

Lichiu – a plum pie – is the quintessential Saxon dish, served for breakfast, lunch or dinner. There is nothing that can't be celebrated with it, nor a tourist who can't be impressed by it. Caroline Fernolend used to serve every potential business investor *papanași* and *lichiu* alongside a little glass of plum brandy,
since this is the traditional way of welcome.

Villages along the 'Saxon belt' have their own particular versions of the recipe, which is remarkable given the small size of the region. The main variations are to be found in the topping, which can be salty or sweet, starting from a simple crème fraîche to layers of semolina cream and fresh fruit (especially plums).

Traditionally, the dairy component was produced at home from buffalo milk; Saxons being famous for rearing buffalo cattle. An interesting choice of herd, buffalo were brought from Egypt in the 18th century by an extraordinary Saxon: Baron von Brukenthal. His story can be found on page 181.

Saxon Plum Pie

Lichiu săsesc cu prune de la Criț

✕ ✕ ✕ ✕ ✕ ✕ ✕ ✕ ✕ ✕ ✕ ✕ ✕ ✕ ✕ ✕ ✕ ✕ ✕

Lichiu is the name for a thin, open pie enriched with eggs, butter and milk, which is baked at a low temperature. This ensures that you get the famous blistered-cream 'blossoms' on the top, like an embroidery of caramelised dots and patches, the pride and glory of any baker. I tried different versions of this when I was in the Saxon area. One of the recipes was baked by my host, Sorina Matei Vonu from Folberth Guesthouse in the Saxon village of Criț, using only produce from her farm. This recipe was adapted to represent one of many variations.

Serves 8

200 g (7 oz/1⅔ cups) plain flour
3 g (½ sachet) fast-action
    dried yeast
50 g (2 oz/¼ cup) caster
    (superfine) sugar
5 tablespoons full-fat milk
1 medium egg, plus 1 yolk
1½ tablespoons unsalted
    butter, softened

For the semolina cream topping

150 ml (5 fl oz/scant ⅔ cup)
    full-fat milk
35 g (1¼ oz/3 tablespoons)
    golden caster
    (superfine) sugar
40 ml (1½ fl oz/scant
    3 tablespoons) honey
45 g (1¾ oz/⅓ cup) semolina
finely grated zest of 1 large lemon
2 egg whites (keep the yolks
    for later)

To finish

150 g (5 oz/¾ cup) full-fat
    crème fraîche
2 egg yolks
350 g (12 oz) plums, halved
    or sliced
ground cinnamon, for sprinkling
icing (confectioner's) sugar,
    for dusting

To make the dough, combine the flour and yeast in a mixing bowl and set aside.

Dissolve the sugar in the milk in a small pan over a low heat just for a couple of minutes. Ensure it is not too hot, then mix in the egg and yolk. Pour it over the flour and yeast and knead until smooth, then add the butter in two stages, kneading well after each addition. I do everything by hand, as the quantities are small. Cover and leave to rest in a warm place while you prepare the topping.

Make the semolina cream topping by bringing the milk, sugar and honey to the boil in a medium pan. Reduce the heat and whisk in the semolina, simmering until the milk is completely absorbed. Mix in the lemon zest, then set aside and allow to cool.

Preheat the oven to 160°C (non-fan)/320°F/gas 2. Grease and line a deep baking tin (pan), 32 x 24 cm (12½ x 9½ in).

Beat the egg whites until foamy, then whisk into the semolina mixture just before you are ready to assemble the pie.

In a separate bowl, combine the crème fraîche with the egg yolks.

Thinly roll out the dough to the size of the tin and press it evenly onto the base of the tin to reach all corners. Prick the dough with a fork, especially at the edges. Spread the semolina cream topping evenly on top, then add the plum halves or slices in rows without overlapping. Dot the crème fraîche mixture on top and gently spread it as evenly as possible. It should not cover the plums entirely.

Bake on the lower shelf of the oven for 50 minutes–1 hour until the top caramelises.

Allow to cool in the tin for 5 minutes, then transfer to a wire cooling rack and slide the baking paper from underneath. Sprinkle with cinnamon. Serve at room temperature, dusted with icing sugar. It tastes just as good the next day too.

Chapter 3
Yeasted

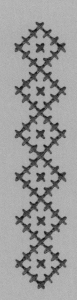

In Romania, there are many festivities and special occasions that are reflected in the kitchen. Since wheat signifies abundance, life giving and resurrection, breads have long been associated with religious and agricultural traditions. Enriched with sugar, butter, milk and eggs, they speak of celebration, gratitude and the hope of good things to come. On these numerous occasions, breadmaking turns into a form of art. Originally, some loaves, sweet or plain, would have had abstract, human-like shapes, anthropomorphical, which in time evolved into a series of braids, twists and loops that were called *păpuși*, 'puppets'.

I recently learned about the variety of ritualistic bread shapes and decorations in Romania. Each region has its own designs, not only specific to each tradition, but also to whether they are meant to be given to adults or children. While many of these breads are made for weddings, Christmas and Easter, others are baked for funerals, distributed as alms and given to carol singers alongside walnuts and apples. Some designs can incorporate as few as ten different shapes and folk motifs, others as many as fifty. The variety is astonishing, not only religious elements, birds, animals and stars, but also items from around the house and farm, such as carts, wheels, horseshoes, scissors, ladders and bridges. Each has its own meaning, and together they almost form a distinct language, 'the language of bread'.

In their simplest forms, festive breads can be round or rectangular featuring a basic braid made of a diagonal cross, whose ends are twisted around each other. When the ends are united in a loop, creating something similar to number 8, the bread is called *colac* or *mucenici*. In this chapter, I have included the iconic *cozonac* bread, *mucenici moldovenești* buns and *poale-n brâu* pies, alongside other regional recipes.

I also tell the story of the Banat region, which is just as spectacular but not as famous as its neighbour Transylvania. The focus is on one of many communities that live here, the German-Swabians. I describe how to bake a *guguluf* (as we call it in Romanian), which is a *gugelhupf* with raisins and cranberries, and *cornuri cu mac*, poppy seed and cherry jam crescents. One final recipe belongs to both Swabians and Hungarians, who are very fond of their *bucte*, yeasted dumplings served with vanilla sauce. Called *buchteln* in German and *aranygaluska* in Hungarian, they are not filled with jam as you may find in other recipes, but are left plain and dusted with icing (confectioner's) sugar.

The recipes are easy to make, even if they require patience, as the doughs need time to rise, to develop structure and flavour.

Romanian Festive Bread with Walnuts and Raisins

Cozonac cu nuci și stafide

Cozonac is the Romanian festive bread par excellence, associated with Christmas and Easter. Many regions and families treasure their own versions. The typical shape is a rectangular braid filled either with the popular combination of walnuts and raisins, or with Turkish delight. The name's etymology is most likely related to the Greek *kosona*, a doll resembling a 'baby in a cradle', says food historian Simona Lazăr, since the breads have been linked to religious celebrations since pre-Christian times. Even today, the process of baking *cozonac* is surrounded by superstition. I give you a recipe that requires only a warm room and making the sign of the cross over the loaves before proving, for luck.

Makes 2 medium loaves

600 g (1 lb 5 oz/5 cups) strong bread flour
14 g (2 sachets) fast-action dried yeast
200 ml (7 fl oz/scant 1 cup) full-fat milk, warmed
2 medium eggs, plus 2 yolks (reserve whites for filling)
150 g (5 oz/generous ⅔ cup) golden caster (superfine) sugar
1 tablespoon vanilla extract
150 g (5 oz/⅔ cup) sour cream, at room temperature
grated zest of 1 large orange
80 g (3 oz) unsalted butter, melted
sunflower oil, for greasing

For the filling

150 g (5 oz/1½ cups) walnuts
150 g (5 oz/1¼ cups) sultanas (light golden raisins)
1 tablespoon milk
1 tablespoon orange blossom water
2 egg whites
75 g (2½ oz/⅓ cup) caster (superfine) sugar

For the glaze

1 small egg, beaten

Combine the flour and yeast in a large bowl or a stand mixer fitted with the paddle attachment. Add the warmed milk, then mix well.

In a separate bowl, beat the eggs and yolks with the sugar and vanilla until foamy, then mix in the sour cream and orange zest. Use a wooden spoon or the mixer to incorporate this into the flour mixture. Beat on medium speed for 5–8 minutes until thick strands of dough begin to separate. Start adding the butter, 1 tablespoon at a time, incorporating well after each addition. At this stage, you can change to a dough hook or knead by hand until the dough is smooth and coming away from the sides of the bowl. Transfer the dough to a greased bowl. Cover and let rest for 1½ hours in a warm place.

Meanwhile, make the filling by blitzing the walnuts and sultanas together in a food processor. Add the milk and the orange blossom water and mix well. In a separate bowl, beat the egg whites with the sugar to stiff peaks, then combine with the walnut mixture. Set aside.

Grease and line two 10 x 21 cm (4 x 8¼ in) loaf tins (pans).

Turn the dough onto a lightly oiled work surface, shape it into a log and divide into 4 equal parts. Gently stretch and roll one part to the length of the tin and double its width. Spread with a quarter of the filling mixture and roll it up into a log. Repeat with the second piece of dough, then twist them together, tucking the ends in, if necessary. Place in the tin. Repeat with the other pieces of dough and place in the second tin. Cover and leave to prove for 30 minutes in a warm place.

Meanwhile, preheat the oven to 180°C (non-fan)/350°F/gas 4.

Brush the breads with the beaten egg. Bake on the lower shelf of the oven for 20 minutes, then reduce the temperature to 160°C (non-fan)/320°F/gas 2 and bake for a further 30 minutes until an inserted skewer comes out clean. Cover the tops with foil if they turn too dark.

Leave to cool in the tin, covered with a cloth, for 10 minutes, then remove to a wire rack to cool completely, still covered with a cloth.

Folded Curd Cheese Pies

Poale–n brâu

The emblem of Moldavia in eastern Romania, these folded pies are the pride and glory of every home baker. The name is typical of the Romanian sense of humour. In the countryside, it is part of women's traditional costume to overlay a beautifully decorated half apron, *poale*, over a plain skirt. The women like to lift one of its corners and tuck it behind the waist belt, *brâu*, so that they can move more freely. This folding is similar to the way the corners of the pies are tucked in, hence the witty name 'lifted skirts'.

Makes 16

For the dough

550 g (1 lb 3 oz/4¼ cups) plain (all-purpose) flour, plus extra for dusting

80 g (3 oz/⅓ cup) caster (superfine) sugar

7 g (1 sachet) fast-action dried yeast

300 ml (10 fl oz/1¼ cups) full-fat milk, slightly warmed

3 egg yolks

125 g (4 oz) unsalted butter, melted and slightly warm

For the filling

100 g (3½ oz/scant ½ cup) set curd cheese, cottage cheese or ricotta, drained of liquid

100 g (3½ oz/scant ½ cup) full-fat cream cheese

1 egg yolk

25 g (¾ oz/2 tablespoons) caster (superfine) sugar

25 g (¾ oz/¼ cup) wheat semolina

2 teaspoons vanilla bean paste

zest of 1 lemon

For the glaze

1 small egg, beaten

To make the dough, mix all the ingredients together in a bowl, apart from the butter. As the dough starts to come together, add the butter little by little, incorporating well after each addition. Knead until smooth and silky, then cover and leave to prove for 1 hour in a warm place.

Meanwhile, make the filling by combining all the ingredients in a bowl.

Line a 24 x 32 x 6 cm (9½ x 12½ x 2¼ in) baking tray or roasting tin (pan).

Flour your work surface and roll out the dough to a 40 cm (16 in) square. Cut the dough into 4 equal parts vertically, then into 4 equal parts horizontally. Place a teaspoonful of the filling in the middle of a piece of dough. Bring the opposite diagonal corners of the dough to overlap in the middle, then bring the other corners into the middle in the same way. Press them well in the middle to seal. The pie should look round as opposed to rectangular, and quite small, but that's fine. Transfer to the baking tray and repeat with the rest of the dough, leaving a small gap between the pies to expand. Cover and leave to prove for 30 minutes in a warm place.

Meanwhile, preheat the oven to 180°C (non-fan)/350°F/gas 4.

Brush the pies evenly with the egg glaze, then bake for 30 minutes on the lower shelf of the oven. Cover with foil if the folds on the pies start to look too dark.

Allow to cool in the tray for 10 minutes, then transfer to a wire cooling rack. I like to eat these slightly warm, as they are best the day they are baked.

Little Saints – Moldavian Saffron Buns

Mucenici Moldovenesti cu șofran

Many dishes in Romania are surrounded by religious stories, and this is one of the most heart-warming. Celebrated on 9 March, this day sees Romanians from all over the world eating these sticky-soft brioche buns, which are soaked in honey syrup and sprinkled with walnuts. The buns are specific to eastern Romania and in fact the dish has a sibling, dividing the country in two. You can find the legend and the other side of the story on page 126.

Makes 8

For the dough
225 ml (8 fl oz/scant 1 cup) full-fat milk
2 pinches of saffron
420 g (15 oz/3 cups) strong bread flour, plus extra for dusting
60 g (2¼ oz/¼ cup) caster (superfine) sugar
7 g (1 sachet) fast-action dried yeast
2 large egg yolks
1 teaspoon vanilla bean paste
90 g (3¼ oz) unsalted butter, melted

For the glaze
1 egg mixed with a drop of milk

For the syrup
400 ml (13 fl oz/generous 1½ cups) water
125 g (4 oz/½ cup) golden caster (superfine) sugar
zest and juice of 1 lemon
1 teaspoon vanilla bean paste
1 tablespoon orange blossom water (optional)

For the topping
3 tablespoons runny honey
75 g (2½ oz/⅔ cup) finely ground walnuts
finely grated zest of 1 lemon

Warm the milk in a small pan and add the saffron, then set aside to cool and infuse for 20 minutes.

In a mixing bowl, combine all the remaining dough ingredients, apart from the butter. Knead until the dough comes away from the sides of the bowl, then gradually add the butter, incorporating well after each addition. Cover and leave to rest in a warm place for 1 hour.

Turn the dough out onto a lightly floured surface and divide into 8 parts. Roll each piece into a log, 40–50 cm (16–20 in) long, bring the ends together in a circle and seal, then twist in the middle to make a figure-of-8 shape. Place each on a lined baking sheet as you go, leaving a little space between them. Cover and leave to prove for 30 minutes in a warm place.

Meanwhile, preheat the oven to 200°C (non-fan)/400°F/gas 6.

Brush the breads with the egg glaze and bake for 30 minutes, or until golden brown. Allow to cool completely.

To make the syrup, bring the water and sugar to the boil in a small pan, then simmer for 10 minutes. Remove from the heat and stir in the rest of the syrup ingredients.

When the *mucenici* have cooled completely, soak them in the syrup for 3 minutes. Transfer to a plate, drizzle with honey and cover them generously with ground walnuts and lemon zest. Serve with more walnuts and honey on the side, so that people can adjust the toppings to their personal preference.

Orange Gugelhupf with Cranberries

Guguluf cu merișoare

+ + + + + + + + + + + + + + + + + + + +

This is a recipe from Banat, western Romania, specific to the areas populated by German communities. It uses yeast, as would have been the case in traditional recipes, and has the feel and texture of an enriched bread rather than a soft cake. Although raisins are considered to be the only authentic filling, I think that many other dried fruits work just as well. I have become rather fond of the tanginess of cranberries, especially since the berries also grow in the Carpathian mountains.

Serves 12

175 g (6 oz) unsalted butter, softened, plus extra for greasing
1 tablespoon fine semolina or plain (all-purpose) flour, for dusting the tin
80 g (3 oz/scant ½ cup) caster (superfine) sugar
4 medium eggs
350 g (12 oz/2¾ cup) plain (all-purpose) flour, plus 1 tablespoon for dusting the fruit
10 g (1½ sachets) fast-action dried yeast
zest of 2 oranges, plus 4 tablespoons of their juice
200 g (7 oz/generous 1½ cups) dried cranberries
50 g (2 oz/scant ½ cup) golden raisins (sultanas)

For the glaze

1 egg yolk mixed with 1 tablespoon water

Grease and sprinkle the inside of a bundt tin (pan) or tall cake tin, 22 cm (9 in) in diameter, with semolina or flour.

In a mixing bowl or stand mixer fitted with the paddle attachment, cream the butter with the sugar, then add the eggs one at a time, alternating with 1 tablespoon of the flour after each addition (don't worry if the mixture looks split). Mix in the remaining flour, yeast, orange zest and juice, scraping down the sides of the bowl a few times. Beat the mixture for 5 minutes on medium speed.

Toss the dried fruit in 1 tablespoon of flour, then add to the dough, ensuring the fruit is evenly distributed. Scrape the dough into the prepared tin and spread and level it with the back of a spoon. Cover with clingfilm (plastic wrap) and leave to rise in a warm place for 2 hours until doubled in size.

Preheat the oven to 190°C (non-fan)/375°F/gas 5.

Brush the top of the *gugelhupf* with the egg glaze and bake on the lower shelf of the oven for 10 minutes, then reduce the heat to 170°C (non-fan)/340°F/gas 3 and bake for a further 25-30 minutes. Insert a skewer into the middle of the cake; if it comes out clean, the cake is ready.

Allow to cool in the tin for 30 minutes, then remove and transfer to a wire cooling rack to cool completely. It's delicious eaten on the same day, but keeps well for up to 3 days.

Banat Swabians
Șvabii din Banat

✖ ✖ ✖ ✖ ✖ ✖ ✖ ✖ ✖ ✖ ✖ ✖ ✖ ✖ ✖ ✖ ✖ ✖ ✖

The story of Banat is one of a long coexistence between many different cultural communities in south-west Romania. Throughout the centuries of Hungarian, Turkish and Habsburg rule, the land was inhabited by four main ethnic groups: Romanians, Serbs, Swabians and Magyars, while the region had also been home to Bulgarians, Jews, Turks, Croatians, Italians, Czechs and the French.

An experiment of social unification

After the Ottoman Empire was pushed out of Banat in the 18th century, Vienna decided to strengthen the border, repopulate it and make profitable a rich land that had been seriously neglected during so many years of war. Known as hard-working and industrious farmers, German settlers were invited to the region from Swabia, Alsace, Bavaria, Nuremberg and the Rhine regions. In the countryside, they spoke different German dialects, which eventually merged into the '*Banat schwowisch*', șvăbesc dialect.

Meanwhile, craftsmen and tradesmen from Vienna and Bohemia settled in the cities, where they spoke a totally different German, an intriguing fact that contributed to a language rift between urban and rural communities. Vienna decided to use a different approach to governance from the one in Transylvania, and pursued an enlightened experiment not based on exemptions or exclusions but aiming to unify a nation through education and ethnic tolerance. They opened schools in the countryside in mixed languages, allowed different religions to coexist and invited different ethnic groups to take part in administration.

A symphony of culinary landscapes

While the cuisine of the region reflected this rich variety, the Swabians excelled at cakes and desserts. *Gugelhupf, kipferl, kolacs, buchtel*, yeasted strudels … all these breads were introduced by the bakers in Bohemia and Slovakia, which for centuries had been part of the Habsburg empire. The recipes were considered routine baking, everyday fare, baked on those Sundays when 'no guests were invited'. On special occasion and visits, Swabians baked layered cakes with buttercream, an unparalleled collection so impressive that at weddings there was a special ceremony for their presentation. These recipes were adopted by many other nations of the Empire, and today are also considered to be traditional Romanian, Serbian, Jewish or Saxon recipes.

Rosemary sprigs and the Swabian wedding cook

To be a wedding cook was one of the most prestigious roles in the community. Selected from among the very talented women cooks of the village, these ladies would perfect their skills by training with professional chefs and confectioners. Their cakes, patisserie and desserts were a form of art, as were the other traditional dishes served on such occasions. The weddings were the most joyful moments in the village life.

Wedding invitations were sent as labels tied with colourful ribbons around bottles of wine and small boxes of baked treats. Little marzipan cookies, almond biscuits, meringues and vanilla shortbreads were carefully decorated and packed. Each was adorned with a little drawing of a rosemary bouquet, with as many sprigs as number of guests invited. They must have been a work of love as weddings could have two to three hundred guests! Interestingly, rosemary was used as a symbol of love and loyalty, and was a constant companion through all celebrations of the year, but was not actually used as an ingredient in cooking. The custom was to serve a dish with a rosemary sprig on the side or sing a song holding a sprig in your hand, and even adorn your hat with it, but not to use its piney aroma in dishes.

Wedding cooks had to know the culinary traditions related to each festivity as they were invited to cook for all the events in the village. The ladies had an aura of kitchen goddesses. Usually, they passed down their skills to their daughters, who learned on the job the art of piped lattices, set creams, multi-tonal layer cakes and sugar roses, so they could follow in their mothers' footsteps.

One such daughter of an exceptional wedding cook and baker was Olga Farca, who started to publish a series of books about the Swabian cuisine from the Banat region in 1989. They resonated deeply with many Swabians around the world, longing to recapture the atmosphere of their long-lost, idyllic village life. After the Second World War, deportations and oppressions saw their numbers thinning in Romania, and many more left after the fall of the Communist regime.

I managed to get in touch with a few Banat Swabians in Germany. Elisabeth Schöps left her village Cărpiniş-Gertianosch in 1988, only one year before the collapse of the regime. The village was situated 10 miles from the frontier and everybody knew the guards and policemen. With a 'limited traffic' pass, Elisabeth crossed the border by train into Serbia, then caught a bus to Kikinda, where she spent the night hidden in the house of a German lady, Tanti Mari. The Serbs had the reputation of sending back Romanians caught crossing in return for money from the authorities.

While she was telling me the story, her husband Andreas put a few books on the table and I could see that they had the entire collection of Olga Farca's recipes. 'Every Swabian has these books. When you cook, you remember the family and your home and only the good times,' said Elisabeth. 'We don't make very sweet cakes these days. I prefer to bake *kipferl* and *kugelhopf* with dried fruit, and only add sugar more as a flavouring.'

I asked her grandson, Patrick Polling, who is the Chairman of the German Banat Youth and Traditional Costume Group, if he spoke Romanian. He didn't. Nor did the others. I could see that the younger generations of Swabians had moved on. Today, they are German and perfectly integrated here, and the past is a memory. They keep their traditions alive through festivals and get togethers, wearing traditional costumes, dancing Swabian folk dances and baking traditional recipes, but they have only visited the Banat a few times. This is typical of the German communities from the diaspora. Not many return. I asked Patrick what he baked. He told me that in his group they bake *kipferl*, the yeasted breads filled with poppy seeds or walnuts, crisp on the outside and with the soft filling in the middle. They are the taste of childhood and homecoming and celebrations.

Meanwhile, Romanians who live in Swabian villages are re-enacting Swabian traditions, including the Church Festival, *Kerweih*, dances and customs. But there are not many Swabians left.

A word about the Swabians who left

The nationalistic sentiments of each ethnic group in the Banat region surged at the beginning of the 20th century. The end of the First World War saw the region divided between Romania, Serbia and Hungary, as it is to this day. After the Second World War, tens of thousands of Swabians were deported to forced labour camps in

Russia on Stalin's orders, leaving behind homes, farmland, animals and even the pot of soup still simmering on the stove. Some of them returned, but to a life that was not their own, only to be deported again by the political regime to one of the most arid and harshest areas of Romania: Bărăgan. Left in the field under the torrid sun with only some pots and pans, duvets and cushions, they were promised 'some wood' by the authorities to start building their homes. They built their villages from the ground with their own hands, house by house, and lived there for many years.

Germany agreed to pay ten thousand Deutschmarks per person to get them out of Romania, and the Communist regime seized this business opportunity with both hands, increasing the price to twenty thousand. This is how the thinning of Swabian communities started even before the fall of the regime, when almost everyone left to return to the Fatherland.

However, many in Germany had no idea who they were, didn't understand why people from Romania spoke German, and the Swabians had to go through yet another process of integration. Only in the last 20 years, through their own newspapers and media, have their stories started to emerge.

I debated whether a book about baking was the place for such a story, but decided I couldn't just write about cakes, cookies and cultural identities, where these very same identities had been deeply affected by recent history. Food has always been a cohesive element, more than just 'bringing friends and family together', it has been vital in keeping the spirit of a culture alive. The enthusiastic group of young Swabians is re-anchoring those memories to something more positive and a future in Germany away from their ancestral lands. And for this I gladly join them for a poppy seed *kipferl* and a slice of *kugelhopf*.

Banat Swabian Poppy Seed and Cherry Jam Crescents

Cornuri din Banat cu mac și gem de cireșe

✗ ✗ ✗ ✗ ✗ ✗ ✗ ✗ ✗ ✗ ✗ ✗ ✗ ✗ ✗ ✗ ✗

These are also known as Pressburger or Bratislava crescents, having derived from a type of strudel made with yeasted dough rather than filo pastry. Many countries and communities in Eastern Europe share similar recipes, whether in the shape of crescents or larger rolls known as *beigli*.

Makes 8

350 g (12 oz/2¾ cups) plain (all-purpose) flour, plus extra for dusting
60 g (2¼ oz) unsalted butter, diced and softened
50 g (2 oz/¼ cup) caster (superfine) sugar
1 medium egg, plus 1 egg yolk
7 g (1 sachet) fast-action dried yeast
100 ml (3½ fl oz/scant ½ cup) full-fat milk

For the filling

75 ml (2½ fl oz/5 tablespoons) double (heavy) cream
100 g (3½ oz/⅔ cup) ground poppy seeds
75 g (2½ oz/¼ cup) cherry jam
zest of 1 lemon

For the glaze

1 medium egg, beaten

In a bowl, mix the flour and the butter with a fork until crumbly. Stir in the sugar, egg and yolk, yeast and milk.

Turn out onto a floured work surface and bring the dough together by hand, kneading until smooth. Return it to the bowl, cover and allow to rest at room temperature for 30 minutes.

Make the filling by warming all the ingredients in a small milk pan over a medium heat. Keep stirring until you can't see any traces of cream and the mixture loosens, becoming spreadable. It needs to be a thick paste, otherwise it will produce steam while baking, and split the crescents. Allow to cool.

Flour your work surface lightly and line a baking sheet with baking paper. Divide the dough into 8 pieces and roll each out to an oval shape, 20-25 cm (8-10 in) in length. Place 2 teaspoons of the filling along one of the longer edges, then roll it up tightly across the width of the oval. Press to seal and gently roll each crescent again keeping your hands on the ends to make them slightly thinner and bringing the ends around like a horseshoe. Place the crescents on the baking sheet, brush with some of the egg glaze and place in the refrigerator for 30 minutes. Brush again with the glaze and return to the refrigerator for a further 30 minutes.

Preheat the oven to 190°C (non-fan)/375°F/gas 5.

Bake for 18 minutes until they turn a deep, golden colour. If they colour too quickly, place a piece of foil loosely over the top.

Remove from the oven and transfer to a wire cooling rack after a few minutes. While you can serve them cold, I like to enjoy their crust and moreish filling when slightly warm.

Golden Dumplings with Ginger Sauce

Găluște aurii cu sos de ghimbir

These dumplings rank highly on the list of favourite dishes of Hungarians and German-Swabians in Romania, evoking memories of childhood, visits to grandparents and home baking. They are yeasted buns, airy and soft, dusted with icing (confectioner's) sugar and served with a delicate vanilla sauce. Hungarians like to sprinkle their *aranygaluska* with chopped walnuts, while German-Swabians leave their *bucte* (*buchteln*) plain. Both recipes evolved side by side, and it is believed that Hungarian emigrants took them to the US, inspiring the creation of monkey bread. I use ginger in the vanilla sauce for its warm flavour, since it was popular in the past in Romanian cooking.

Serves 6

For the dough

350 g (12 oz/2¾ cups) plain
 (all-purpose) flour
7 g (1 sachet) fast-action
 dried yeast
125 ml (4 fl oz/½ cup)
 full-fat milk
2 medium eggs
3 tablespoons caster
 (superfine) sugar
1 tablespoon rum
1 teaspoon vanilla bean paste
3 tablespoons melted butter,
 plus 1½ tablespoons for
 brushing and greasing

For the sauce

300 ml (10 fl oz/1¼ cups)
 full-fat milk
3 medium egg yolks
3 tablespoons caster
 (superfine) sugar
4 teaspoons plain
 (all-purpose) flour
2 teaspoons vanilla extract
1 teaspoon ground ginger,
 or more if preferred

icing (confectioner's) sugar,
 for dusting

In a mixing bowl or a stand mixer fitted with a dough hook, mix together all the dough ingredients apart from the butter and knead until they form a soft dough. Add the 3 tablespoons of melted butter little by little, incorporating it well after each addition. Knead for 5 minutes, then cover and leave to rise in a warm place for 1 hour.

Butter a deep baking dish, 20 cm (8 in) in diameter. Tear off a 50 g (2 oz) piece of the dough and form into a ball. Roll it briefly in the remaining melted butter and place it in the dish. Repeat with the rest of the dough, arranging the balls in the dish in a circular fashion with one in the middle. Cover and leave to prove in a warm place for 30 minutes until doubled in size.

Meanwhile, preheat the oven to 180°C (non-fan)/350°F/gas 4.

Bake for 25-30 minutes until golden brown on top.

Remove from the oven and set aside while you make the sauce.

Put the milk in a pan and bring to a gentle simmer. In a bowl, beat the yolks with the rest of the sauce ingredients to a runny consistency. Slowly pour the milk over the yolks, stirring constantly, then transfer the mixture back into the pan. Simmer over a low heat, without boiling, until the sauce thickens slightly.

To serve, lightly dust the buns with icing sugar. Place a bun in the middle of a plate and pour the sauce around it. Serve warm and allow two per person.

Chapter 4
Strudels and Pastry

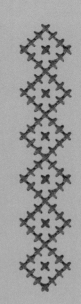

For centuries the pastries in Romania were influenced by Middle Eastern and Balkan cuisines, with their varieties of syrupy filo desserts, nutty halvas and rose-scented Turkish delight. Later came the Austrian-German influence and with it our love for thin strudels and jam tarts.

Elisabeth Luard wrote in her book *European Peasant Cookery* that the journey of strudel started when 'the Turkish pastry chef met the German housewife'. In a country like Romania, where both the Turkish and Austrian empires shared a border right through the middle of it, these influences fused into the variety of dishes we find here today. Although the Ottomans were world-renowned for making an art form of filo desserts, it's fair to assume that skilful Armenian and Greek bakers living in different parts of what is today Romania cast their own spell over our cuisine too.

When we travel to Transylvania and Banat, regions that were ruled in turn by both the Ottoman and Habsburg Empires, it is clear that a strudel sits at the centre of the culinary traditions of many communities. Halrun Reinholz, a German-Swabian born in Timișoara, fondly remembers the 'strudel days' of her childhood, where meals would start with a hearty, clear soup and continue with both savoury and sweet strudels.

For the ones in this book, I'm using two different recipes from my maternal grandmother, which she learned as a girl growing up in Transylvania. The key to making a strudel lies in the dough flexibility, which is built by alternating kneading with resting. When it comes to stretch and pull, it only takes a few minutes for you to get the hang of it, then you gain confidence and it's very easy to do. You can of course buy filo, but often these sheets are dry and break easily. You can use a good brand from an international food shop or bought online, but you will miss the beauty of handling filo dough.

French-style tarts with a crisp, buttery base and custard fillings don't feature prominently in the Romanian baking repertoire. Although imports occured during the last century, they remained on the sidelines. Instead, we prefer a Linzer-style tart, with a more cake-like crumb and made with jam.

Last but not least, what we call puff pastry, *foitaj*, follows an intriguing method when made at home. The butter needs to be soft, warm and spreadable. A recipe that I grew very fond of while testing it for this book (*Haioș* on page 110) is a good one one for practising this technique.

In this chapter, I also tell the story of the pomegranate blossoms in the Armenian Quarter in Bucharest, and of this remarkable community in Romania. Their recipe for *pakhlava* is a celebration of filo pastry and the Armenian national fruit, the pomegranate.

Strudels and Pastry

Pumpkin Strudel

Ştrudel cu dovleac

Ştrudele have always been my favourite desserts and I have fond memories of making them with my grandmother, stretching and pulling the pastry over the dining table. There are two fillings that are considered traditional, either apple or curd cheese, but my grandmother used to make seasonal ones too, with deep-flavoured pumpkin in the autumn and sour cherries in the summer. I am sure that many other people did the same. She never threw away the dough trimmings, but would tear them into small pieces and simmer them in a soup or stew.

Serves 6–8

For the dough
(see also note on page 99)
300 g (10½ oz/2½ cups) strong bread flour, plus extra for dusting
scant 2 tablespoons sunflower oil
1 tablespoon verjuice or white wine vinegar
1 medium egg, lightly beaten
120 ml (4 fl oz/½ cup) lukewarm water
1 pinch of salt

For the filling
700 g (1 lb 9 oz) pumpkin flesh, grated
3 tablespoons honey
40 g (1½ oz/3½ tablespoons) caster (superfine) sugar
1 teaspoon vanilla extract
1 teaspoon ground cinnamon

Alternative fillings
For apple, use recipe on page 57
For cheese, use recipe on page 62

For brushing
70 g (2½ oz) unsalted butter, melted, mixed with 2 tablespoons sunflower oil

In a mixing bowl, combine all the dough ingredients and knead until the dough comes away from the sides of the bowl. Cover and rest at room temperature for 15 minutes, then knead again for 2 minutes. Repeat this process twice in order to develop the right elasticity in the dough. After this, rest the dough for 1 hour. You can also make it the day before and rest it in the refrigerator, in which case bring the dough to room temperature before stretching it.

To make the filling, combine all the ingredients and set aside.

Preheat the oven to 190°C (non-fan)/375°F/gas 5. Line your largest baking tray (pan) with baking paper.

It is helpful to use a kitchen table for this next stage, with room to move around it. Mine is 120 x 90 cm (4 x 3 ft). Cover it with a clean tablecloth and sprinkle generously with flour, rubbing it into the cloth. Place the dough in the middle and use a lightly dusted rolling pin to roll out from the middle in all directions. Ensure the dough doesn't stick to the cloth; keep turning it and flouring the cloth. When the dough is too large to roll, gently slide the back of your hands underneath it, as close as possible to the cloth, and start pulling the dough towards you while you open your arms slightly. Use your fingertips to lift, hold and stretch the edges if needed. Make a gentle shaking movement, as though you are stretching a bed sheet. You will soon get a feel for how this works. Go around the edges of the dough repeating these movements. Opaque patches mean the dough is thicker in those areas, so try to focus on them. When you manage to pull the dough over the sides of your table or as thin as possible, use scissors to trim off the thick edges. Drizzle half of the butter mixture evenly on top. Divide the filling in half and arrange evenly along the two longer sides. Lift one side of the tablecloth to help you roll one side of the strudel halfway up to enclose the filling, then repeat with the opposite side. Use a knife to separate the rolls where they meet in the middle. Trim the ends. Loosely zig-zag one roll into the baking tray, then repeat with the other roll, continuing the zig-zag on. Brush very gently with the remaining butter mixture.

Bake for 30 minutes, or until golden brown.

Serve warm but not hot.

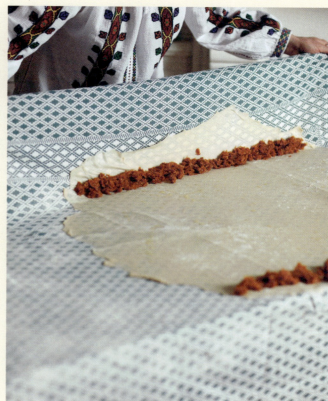

Transylvanian Cherry Strudel

Reteș din Transilvania cu cireșe

This pastry is made with butter and requires a very warm room when handling it. It is called *reteș*, which is the Hungarian name for strudel. This is the recipe that my grandmother always used with a cherry filling, perhaps because this is how she was taught to make it.

Serves 6–8

For the dough
(see also note below)
300 g (10½ oz/2½ cups)
    strong bread flour
3½ tablespoons unsalted
    butter, softened
1 tablespoon verjuice or white
    wine vinegar
150 ml (5 fl oz/scant ⅔ cup)
    lukewarm water

For the filling
500 g (1 lb 2 oz) cherries, halved
50 g (2 oz/¼ cup) caster sugar
50 g (2 oz/scant ½ cup)
    semolina

For brushing
70 g (2½ oz) unsalted butter,
    melted, mixed with
    2 tablespoons sunflower oil

To glaze after baking
4 teaspoons plain
    yoghurt diluted with
    1 tablespoon water

In a mixing bowl, combine 50 g (2 oz/scant ½ cup) of the flour with the soft butter to a thick cream consistency. Add the remaining dough ingredients and knead well until the dough is soft and silky. Cover and leave to rest in a warm place for 10 minutes (an oven that has been heated to 60–70°C/140–158°F/gas ¼ and turned off is ideal). Knead again, then repeat this process twice more. Rest it for a final 20 minutes before starting to stretch. If the room is not warm enough, warm a bowl in the oven, then turn it over the dough like a dome and leave for 5 minutes before starting.

Make the filling by combining all the ingredients in a bowl. Set aside.

Preheat the oven to 190°C (non-fan)/375°F/gas 5. Line your largest baking tray (pan) with baking paper.

Use the method in the previous recipe on page 96 to stretch and pull the dough. Fill with the cherry filling, then roll all the way up. Cut the strudel into pieces that fit the length of your baking tray (you should get about 4). Pull a little of the dough over the cut ends of each strudel and seal. Place each strudel on the tray next to one another and brush with the butter mixture.

Bake for 30 minutes, or until golden brown. Immediately after you remove the strudels from the oven, brush with the yoghurt mixture and cover with a clean cloth. Leave to cool for 15 minutes, then serve.

Note

If you decide to buy filo pastry, use a packet of 12 sheets. Place 3 sheets next each another on a large dish towel, overlapping the edges, so that they match the length of your baking tray. Drizzle with the butter and oil mixture, then place a quarter of the filling along the longer side and use the cloth to help you roll it all the way up. Seal the edges and transfer the strudel to the baking tray. Repeat with the remaining pastry sheets and filling, placing the strudels loosely next to each other. Brush the tops again with butter and bake.

Strudels and Pastry

Vanilla and Egg Liqueur Slice

Cremșnit cu lichior de ouă

Recipes for *cremșnit* can be found in many countries that once belonged to the Habsburg Empire, and Romania is no exception, it being one of our favourite desserts. There are many variations starting from the pastry layers – either puff or shortcrust – to the fillings – sometimes vanilla custard, whipped cream or a fruity meringue. In this recipe, I give you a version with shortcrust pastry and an egg liqueur and vanilla filling. Egg liqueur is popular in many desserts across the former Empire. For a non-alcoholic version, spread the base layer with raspberry, apricot or rosehip jam, for an additional flavour.

Makes 8

For the pastry

120 g (4 oz) unsalted butter, softened, plus extra for greasing

60 g (2½ oz/¼ cup) golden caster (superfine) sugar

1 medium egg

220 g (8 oz/1¾ cups) plain (all-purpose) flour, plus extra for dusting

½ teaspoon baking powder

For the filling

350 ml (12 fl oz/scant 1½ cups) full-fat milk

180 ml (6 fl oz/¾ cup) double (heavy) cream

3 large eggs, separated

80 g (3 oz/⅓ cup) golden caster (superfine) sugar

2 heaped tablespoons plain (all-purpose) flour

3½ tablespoons unsalted butter

80 ml (2½ fl oz/5 tablespoons) egg liqueur (advocaat or eier-likör)

2 teaspoons vanilla bean paste

2 teaspoons vanilla extract

3 gelatine leaves

2–3 tablespoons icing (confectioner's) sugar

First, make the filling. Heat the milk and cream in a large pan. Combine the egg yolks with the sugar and flour in a large bowl. While the milk is warming, transfer a few tablespoons into the yolk mixture, whisking it to a cream consistency. Pour the rest of the hot milk over the yolks, in a steady stream, whisking all the time. Transfer the custard back into the pan and cook over a medium heat until thick. Leave to cool for 10 minutes, then whisk in the butter, egg liqueur and vanillas.

Soak the gelatine leaves in a bowl of cold water for 5 minutes, then remove and add them to the lukewarm custard. Mix well, then leave to cool.

Whisk the egg whites to stiff peaks, then fold the custard little by little into the whites until you have a smooth consistency. Set aside.

To make the pastry, cream the butter with the sugar in a large bowl until pale, then mix in the egg. Add the flour and baking powder and combine well with a fork until it resembles coarse breadcrumbs. Bring the dough together by hand without kneading, then cover the bowl and refrigerate for 10 minutes.

Preheat the oven to 200°C (non-fan)/400°F/gas 6. Grease and line the base of a 18 x 24 x 6 cm (7 x 9½ x 2¼ in) baking tray (pan).

Flour the work surface and divide the pastry into two equal parts, keeping one in the refrigerator. Roll the other out to the size of the baking tray, then place it in the baking tray.

Bake for 12 minutes.

Remove the baked pastry sheet from the tray and set it aside. Line the baking tray once again, and repeat the rolling and baking process with the second half of the pastry to create a second layer. Slice one of the pastry sheets into 8 rectangles while still warm. Leave to cool.

When the layers have cooled, line the baking tray with clingfilm (plastic wrap) and place the unsliced pastry sheet on the base.

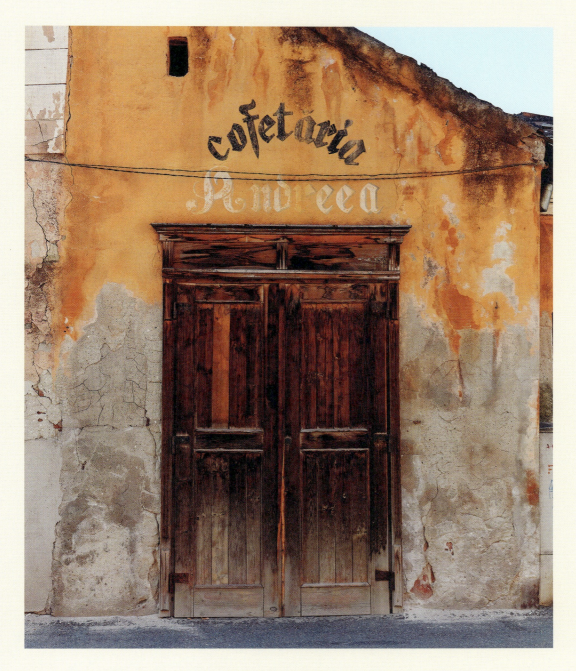

Pour over the custard and place it in the refrigerator to firm up slightly. Rearrange the 8 slices of pastry on top when the cream is set enough to hold them. Cover with another layer of clingfilm and return the tray to the refrigerator for at least 2 hours or overnight.

With the help of the clingfilm, lift the set pastry out of the tray. Slice into 8 pieces all the way through, dust with icing sugar and serve.

Strudels and Pastry

Lemon Verbena Cataif with Honey Cream

Cataif cu frișcă

+ +

As unlikely as it may seem to find a *kadayif* or *cataif* recipe in a book about Romania, centuries of Ottoman rule have left their mark on our cuisine in many ways, including these syrup-soaked luscious desserts. When I lived in Bucharest, a *cataif* was the realm of professional pastry chefs, with most people buying it readymade in stores. One of my favourites was in an old part of the city, Piața Rossetti, a store famous for its *cataif* made with whipped cream and a lemony, refreshing syrup. I have recreated those flavours in this recipe and included a few leaves of lemon verbena for their subtle, herbal fragrance.

Serves 6

250 g (9 oz) cataif/kataifi pastry (found in Middle Eastern stores or online)
100 g (3½ oz) unsalted butter, melted

For the syrup

250 ml (8½ fl oz/1 cup) water
40 g (1½ oz/3½ tablespoons) caster (superfine) sugar
40 g (1½ oz/2 tablespoons) honey
juice of 1 medium lemon (reserve the zest for the filling, below)
6 small lemon verbena leaves, finely chopped

For the filling

150 g (5 oz/⅔ cup) double (heavy) cream
3 tablespoons icing (confectioner's) sugar
100 g (3½ oz/scant ½ cup) full-fat cream cheese
zest from the above lemon

To serve

honey, for drizzling
2 small lemon verbena leaves, finely chopped

First, make the syrup by bringing the water, sugar and honey to the boil in a pan, then reduce the heat and simmer for 15 minutes. Add the lemon juice and lemon verbena leaves and leave to cool.

Preheat the oven to 180°C (non-fan)/350°F/gas 4.

Separate and fluff up the strands of pastry, placing them in a single layer on a large baking tray (pan). Drizzle evenly with the melted butter and use your fingers to thoroughly coat the strands with it. Bake for 20 minutes, or until the pastry turns golden. Remove from the oven and leave to cool.

Make the filling by whipping the cream with the sugar in a large bowl. Fold it into the cream cheese together with the lemon zest.

Arrange half of the shredded pastry over the base of a 24 x 12 cm (9½ x 5 in) serving dish. Evenly spoon over half of the syrup, then spread the filling on top. Layer the remaining pastry on top, then spoon over the remaining syrup. Allow the flavours to infuse for 1 hour at room temperature (if it's not too hot, but ideally not in the refrigerator).

Portion into 6 slices and scoop them out onto plates. Drizzle with a little honey and sprinkle with chopped lemon verbena leaves.

Pomegranate Blossom in the Armenian Quarter

✖ ✖ ✖ ✖ ✖ ✖ ✖ ✖ ✖ ✖ ✖ ✖ ✖ ✖ ✖ ✖ ✖ ✖ ✖

The Armenian quarter is an old, picturesque part of Bucharest that encapsulates the spirit of its community in the capital city. A couple of centuries ago it was an important merchant district, set up close to one of the city's main open-air markets, being flanked on one side by the longest road in 19th-century Bucharest, Calea Moșilor. Today, you can see the prestigious commercial past in many ornate buildings with stores on the ground floor and generous living spaces above. Other houses sit on the quiet maze of streets, built solely as accommodation, with wild roses climbing up the tall gates and grapevines arching over the entrances to provide shelter from the heat of the summer. You can hear the occasional noise, perhaps a call for lunch, or a dog barking, but then the tranquility returns. You can easily feel cut off from the city, even though you are right in the middle of it.

I know this area well. My sister and her family live in one of the apartment blocks on Calea Moșilor. Parallel rows of apartments were built in the 1980s along both sides of this two-mile avenue, a project of 'urban systematisation' successfully run by the Communist regime, which meant 'demolition by bulldozing'. A lot of the historic town, already devastated by property confiscations and neglect, was lost. What has survived is now hidden behind these concrete structures piled high like tins of sardines.

'I often take a longer route home to stroll along these streets, trying to piece together what I hear from people and see in old photographs with what is now left of it all,' says Paul Agopian, a respected member of the Armenian community. 'One day I realised I had in front of me a few pomegranate trees. They don't have the conditions to bear fruit here in Bucharest, but the flowers are beautiful in spring. They were growing in adjacent gardens, whose owners must have been friends or family, and brought their trees from Armenia. It is an important tree to us and a symbol of our identity.'

I think that the Armenian quarter can still tell the tale of its flourishing past. While communities of Armenians had settled in Moldavia and Transylvania since the 11th century, fleeing different invasions and persecutions, it was only much later that they travelled south, to Wallachia. Greek Phanariote princes from Constantinople were appointed in the 18th century by the Ottoman Empire to rule the Romanian principalities, and they recognised the key role of Armenians in the prosperity of Bucharest. They were given the right to form an organised community here, to elect their own leaders, to build a church, a school and to benefit from a relative fiscal freedom.

Armenians were involved in a variety of trades, from tobacco, delicatessens and coffee shops, to weaving rugs and making leather goods, shoes and luxury clothing for the Royal Court. They were also highly regarded as bakers and were masters of the Guild of Bakers in Bucharest at a time when two in three bakeries tempting their clients with freshly baked breads in the city were Armenian. A similar situation occurred at the markets, where many stalls were hired by Armenian pastry and pie makers, who also sold doughnuts, candy floss, sausages, beer and the so-called *bigi-bigi*, walnut and fruit 'sausages'.

They opened stores and inns all over the city, including the iconic Hanul lui Manuc, luckily still standing today in all its glory near the old 17th-century Royal Court. The inn was the first of its kind in Bucharest, offering not only rooms to sleep in but also space for stores and wholesalers on the ground floor. Manuc Bei was the only Armenian to be given a noble title, immensely rich and lending money to princes, he was suspected to have been a spy for Russia against the Ottoman Empire. It proved to be a dangerous occupation that didn't end well.

While the ruling princes were still fond of Ottoman fashions and lifestyle, they also acquired a taste for the sophisticated, modern dishes of the West. Armenians were there to help, establishing trade networks that shifted goods back and forth between the Ottoman Empire in the east, through Bucharest all the way to Vienna. I read through a list of imports usual for those times that mentioned coffee and sugar, rice and oil, black pepper, ginger called *zingefil*, saffron from Rumalia, cloves, nutmeg, aniseed, pistachios from Damascus, almonds from the Greek Island of Chios, vodka from Trieste, Saxon wines from Brașov in Transylvania, plus oranges, lemons and sultanas. It evokes a picture of a cosmopolitan, effervescent city where the extravagant lifestyles of princes and the nouveau riche boosted its prosperity.

The Armenian street festival

I asked Paul Agopian about *pakhlava* and *cataifs* being absent from the list of treats sold at the markets two centuries ago. 'They are celebration dishes, usually made for weddings and church or festive gatherings. What is specific to our *pakhlava* is the addition of cinnamon and ground cloves. I bake many trays every year for the Armenian Festival, where I keep a stall with my family,' he said. I know that the queue for their *pakhlava* usually goes around the block. He also makes very delicate, rich shortbreads, Armenian *kurabia*, and tells me to add a pinch of mahlep in the recipe for this book (see page 50), for its aromatic cherry flavour.

During the festival, which takes place every August, the entire Armenian quarter is turned into a pedestrian area, with events, traditional dances, book launches and live music taking place all day. Armenians are one of the twenty ethnic groups that have funding from the Romanian government to promote and share their culture and values through events.

'Armenians are very proud of their language, their church and their food,' says Paul, his own story being very powerful. His family found refuge in Romania after surviving the 1915 Armenian Genocide by the Ottoman Empire. Romania was one of the first countries in Europe to accept refugees and many Armenians found a safe home here. He owes his journey into the world of food to both his great grandfather and his grandmother, and to his commitment to understanding Armenian culture. While he had a day job as a financial advisor in a bank, Paul studied to be a professional chef, then for a while cooked in a restaurant every evening after work. He told me: 'The job at the Festival is the hardest, mainly because every year I want to share different dishes that continue the Armenian food story from the previous years.'

The coffee trade

To make a living, Paul's great-grandfather opened a coffee shop in Curtea de Argeş, the former capital of the Wallachian principality. Refugees couldn't find jobs in factories or in agriculture, so they had to own a business or a shop, whether in manufacturing, trading or commerce. Because some merchants had their own roasting machines, they were able to combine technology with their personal flair and traditional knowledge, creating their own famous signature coffee. Even the Romanian Royal House became a loyal customer. In fact, the coffee trade lay almost exclusively in Armenian hands well into the 1970s.

In his shop, Paul Agopian's great-grandfather prepared the coffee in the old way, using large trays full of fine sand, which were placed on the stove to heat up. It was said that he never turned the stoves off. The copper coffee pots were first filled with water, then sunk halfway into the hot sand, so the heat could envelop them evenly. The pots would have been raised or lowered, as required, to adjust the temperature. When the ground coffee was added, it foamed up very quickly, so the pots were removed, then lowered again a few more times. The coffee was strong, with a thick crema foam on top, served in small hand-painted cups, with no milk, and perhaps with a little sugar. The sweetness was adjusted to the customers' liking.

There are a lot of Armenian traditions to be revived, especially in coffee-making and cooking, and I am yet to discover a place in Romania that speaks genuinely of both. What is instead remarkable, is the number of energetic, enthusiastic Armenians throughout the country, whether part of the Union of Armenians or independent groups, who are proud of their roots and happily share their traditions with the rest of our Romanian nation.

Armenian Pakhlava with Pomegranate Syrup

Pakhlava armenească cu sirop de rodii

✕ ✕ ✕ ✕ ✕ ✕ ✕ ✕ ✕ ✕ ✕ ✕ ✕ ✕ ✕ ✕ ✕ ✕ ✕

The recipe here belongs to Paul Agopian and we agreed together that I can use a little pomegranate molasses in the syrup, as I wanted to follow in the footsteps of the preceding story and celebrate this fruit so important to all Armenians.

Makes 16 small slices

For the syrup

300 ml (10 fl oz/1¼ cups) water
200 g (7 oz/scant 1 cup)
    caster (superfine) sugar
60 ml (2 fl oz/¼ cup)
    pomegranate molasses

For the filling

300 g (10½ oz/3 cups) walnuts
1 pinch of salt
2 teaspoons ground cinnamon
2 teaspoons ground cloves

To assemble

2 x packets of 12 filo pastry
    sheets (depending on
    the brand, you can use
    min. 10 to max. 15 sheets
    per packet)
120 g (4 oz) unsalted
    butter, melted
16 whole cloves (optional)

Note

I was told that the name comes from *pak* (Lent) and *lavash* (bread). The dish was originally prepared for breaking Lent and had to have 20 layers of filo at the base and 20 on top of the filling, which totalled the number of Lent days. If you are not making it for religious purposes (and as filo pastry most often comes in packets of 12 sheets), it makes sense to use this number.

First, make the syrup by bringing all the syrup ingredients to the boil in a pan. Reduce the heat to medium and simmer for 15 minutes. Leave to cool.

Next, make the filling. By hand or in a food processor, chop the walnuts with the salt to obtain a coarse consistency. Combine with the cinnamon and ground cloves.

Preheat the oven to 170°C (non-fan)/340°F/gas 3.

Grease a deep baking tray (pan), 20 x 32 cm (8 x 13 in) or a size as close as possible to the size of your filo sheets. If necessary, trim the filo sheets with a pair of scissors. Lay the first 12 sheets in the baking tray, one by one, brushing generously with melted butter each time. Evenly spread the filling mixture on top, then lay the other 12 sheets of filo on top in the same way, brushing with butter as before. Brush the top generously with butter. With a sharp knife, cut the *pakhlava* in half lengthways, all the way through the layers, then cut it widthways into quarters. Cut each resulting rectangle on the diagonal, alternating the direction to create a pattern.

Bake for 30 minutes, then remove from the oven. Using a tablespoon, carefully pour the syrup on top, distributing it evenly. Decorate with whole cloves on top for a more intense flavour, if wished. Allow to cool in the tray, then serve.

Hájas Hungarian Lard Pastries with Plum Jam

Haioş cu prune

Traditionally, these puff pastries use shredded leaf lard to create the beautiful layers, but rendered leaf lard, or a combination of standard lard with butter, works well too. I wanted to include this recipe not only for its prominent place in Transylvanian Hungarian cuisine, but also because it is made with pure fats. As the philosophy of farming and selling meat sustainably gathers momentum, many more butchers are now offering lard, fresh beef suet and tallow. For practical reasons, I tested a combination that is more accessible than leaf lard. I have the recipe from Rebeka Stamate, born in the old spa town of Sovata, and she told me to keep a light hand when rolling the pastry, otherwise the layers don't open fully.

Makes 12

For the prune filling
100 g (3½ oz) prunes
zest and juice of
   1 medium lemon

For the dough
350 g (12 oz/2¾ cups)
   strong bread flour, plus
   extra for dusting
1 medium egg, lightly beaten
5 g (1 teaspoon) salt
2 teaspoons verjuice or vinegar
50 g (2 oz/¼ cup) sour cream
120 ml (4 fl oz/½ cup) water

For the lard mixture
80 g (3 oz) unsalted
   butter, softened
80 g (3 oz) pure lard,
   preferably from a jar,
   at room temperature
1 tablespoon strong bread flour

icing (confectioner's) sugar,
   for dusting

First, make the filling. In a food processor, purée the prunes with the lemon zest and juice to a thick consistency. Add the juice gradually – you may not need it all.

Next, make the dough by mixing all the ingredients in a bowl. Knead until it comes away from the sides of the bowl. Cover and leave to rest for 15 minutes. Repeat this process twice more.

Meanwhile, make the lard mixture. Cream the butter with the lard to a soft, mousse-like consistency. Mix in the flour, then set aside in a warm place without letting it melt.

Briefly knead the dough again before you start to roll it. Roll it out on a lightly floured work surface to a 30 x 40 cm (12 x 16 in) rectangle with the long side closest to you. Keep flouring underneath if it gets too sticky. It is a soft dough, so be gentle and don't press too much on the pastry when rolling. Make sure that the sides of the rectangle are straight. Spread a quarter of the lard mixture over the dough with your fingertips, leaving a little edge around the outside for sealing. Fold the top third in to the middle, then the fold the bottom third over it to cover. Next, bring the right-hand third over to the middle, then fold the left-hand third on top of that so it looks like a book with the spine on the left. Place in the refrigerator for 15–30 minutes until firm but still flexible.

Repeat this rolling, folding and chilling process three more times, adding a further quarter of the lard mixture each time. It is okay if, as you keep rolling, you work with a slightly smaller rectangle. Rest the pastry in the refrigerator overnight.

The next day, allow the dough to rest at room temperature for 20 minutes. Roll out to a 25 x 35 cm (10 x 14 in) rectangle with the short side nearest you. Cut into thirds vertically, then into quarters horizontally. Don't use a slicing movement, but rather one clear,

decisive cut, without dragging the knife, otherwise the edges will seal and will not open. Some people like to heat the knife blade with a blowtorch to ensure a clean cut.

Place 1 teaspoonful of plum filling in the middle of each rectangle. Gently fold one short side of each rectangle over the filling. Try not to lift the pastry by the edges and don't press or seal. Place on a lined baking tray and place back in the refrigerator while you heat the oven.

Preheat the oven to 210°C fan/220°C (non-fan)/430°F/gas 8 (ideally use a fan oven for this recipe).

Bake for 25 minutes on a lower shelf of the oven.

Transfer to a wire rack to cool and dust with icing sugar to serve.

Note

If you find a block of fresh leaf lard to buy, it needs to be shredded first, then whipped to a mousse consistency. Use 160 g (5½ oz) without mixing it with butter.

111

Strudels and Pastry

Linzer Tart with Blackcurrant Jam

Tartă cu gem de coacaze

This type of tart was first mentioned in cookery books printed in Romania in the 19th century and it had an Austrian origin. It was also part of the recipe portfolio that young ladies learned either abroad in finishing schools in Vienna or at home from family cookery notebooks passed from one generation to another. I was lucky to have been sent such a notebook by a friend in Romania. Spanning over 76 years, *Rețetele Herminei* is a collection of recipes started by a well-educated young German woman at the beginning of her married life. Later on, her daughters Minka and Hedwiga added their own recipes, continuing the family tradition. I tested a few versions of this Linzer tart and decided on the ingredients and method below, which take elements from each.

Serves 8

150 g (5 oz) unsalted butter, cold and diced, plus extra for greasing
250 g (9 oz/2 cups) plain (all-purpose) flour
50 g (2 oz/½ cup) ground almonds
60 g (2¼ oz/¼ cup) caster (superfine) sugar
1 teaspoon cocoa powder
2 teaspoons ground cinnamon
2 medium egg yolks
3 tablespoons water or white wine

For the filling

350 g (12 oz) blackcurrant jam (or make your own, see page 261)

Rub the butter into the flour until it resembles breadcrumbs or pulse together in a food processor. Add the rest of the ingredients and mix until the dough sticks together, then turn onto a work surface and bring the dough together by pressing with your fingertips. Try not to knead. Cut 150 g (5 oz) of the dough, wrap each piece separately and place both in the refrigerator for 40 minutes. The dough needs to be firm but still flexible.

Preheat the oven to 170°C (non-fan)/340°F/gas 3. Lightly grease the base of a 30 x 20 x 2 cm (12 x 8 x ¾ in) baking tray (pan).

Use two sheets of baking paper a little larger than the tray and roll out the larger piece of dough between them to roughly the size of the tray. Remove the baking paper on top and place the other sheet together with the dough in the tray. Press with your fingertips until the dough fits the base of the tray, prick it with a fork and place in the refrigerator.

Use the same method to roll out the smaller piece of dough to about the size of the tray. Cut it into 2 cm (¾ in) wide stripes (you could use a fluted pastry cutter for this for an attractive look, if you like). Chill the strips in the refrigerator if they get too soft.

Take the pastry base out of the refrigerator and spread the jam on top of the pastry. Arrange half of the pastry strips diagonally across the jam filling, spacing them equally. Repeat in the opposite direction. Trim the edges if necessary.

Bake for 45-50 minutes.

Transfer to a wire rack to cool for several hours before cutting. I prefer to serve this the next day, when it reaches the perfect consistency and flavour.

Peach Galette with Pistachios

Tartă cu piersici

Although desserts like this only appeared in our cuisine as an import from France in the late 19th and early 20th century, they offer a window into the style of a cosmopolitan society at the beginning of a newly united country. The pistachios would have come via trade routes, with the best ones being imported from Damascus and only available to an exclusive clientele. After the Second World War through to the 1990s, pistachios gradually disappeared from the markets in Romania to the point where we didn't even know what they were, apart from an overly sweet flavour in a pale green ice cream. In this recipe, I'm returning them to their former glory, complementing juicy peaches and flaky, buttery pastry.

Serves 8

For the dough
100 g (3½ oz) unsalted butter
150 g (5 oz/1¼ cups) plain (all-purpose) flour, plus extra for dusting
150 g (5 oz/⅔ cup) sour cream

For the filling
300 g (10½ oz) sliced peaches
2 teaspoons ground nutmeg
50 g (2 oz) shelled pistachios: 30 g (1 oz) chopped and the remainder crushed
1 tablespoon honey

For brushing
1 small egg mixed with 1 teaspoon sour cream

First, make the dough. Gently rub the butter into the flour until it resembles breadcrumbs or use a food processor to combine. Briefly mix in the sour cream. Transfer to a piece of clingfilm (plastic wrap) and bring the dough together by hand, pressing with your fingertips rather than kneading. Wrap in clingfilm, flatten to a disc and place in the refrigerator for 1 hour. It needs to chill but not turn rock solid.

Preheat the oven to 200°C (non-fan)/400°F/gas 6.

Lightly flour the work surface and roll out the pastry to a circle, 25 cm (10 in) in diameter. Place the sliced peaches in the middle of the pastry and sprinkle with the nutmeg, chopped pistachios and honey. Fold the edges of the pastry over the fruit. You don't need to enclose the fruit completely, just create a folded border. Brush the pastry with the egg mixture and sprinkle with the crushed pistachios.

Bake for 40-50 minutes until the pastry looks golden and crisp and the fruit is soft.

Remove from the oven and leave to cool completely before serving.

Vanilla Cream Horns with Strawberries

Cornete cu frișcă și căpșuni

I believe that the beauty of these pastries lies in their simplicity. Although it's possible to make our own puff pastry, I prefer to take a shortcut. Store-bought puff pastry from a good supplier will save you a lot of time. These pastries are very simple and fun to make, and even if you have to buy the pastry moulds you will find you use them again and again. The whipped cream and fresh fruit make a wonderfully light filling.

Makes about 23

unsalted butter, for greasing
plain (all-purpose) flour,
    for dusting
500 g (1 lb 2 oz) ready-rolled
    puff pastry sheet
1 small egg, beaten

For the filling

150 g (5 oz/⅔ cup) double
    (heavy) cream
3 tablespoons icing
    (confectioner's) sugar, plus
    extra for dusting
2 teaspoons vanilla bean paste
150 g (5 oz) strawberries: a few
    diced and the rest sliced

Preheat the oven to 200°C (non-fan)/400°F/gas 6. Lightly grease your conical pastry horn moulds on the outside. Line a baking sheet with baking paper.

Unroll the puff pastry sheet, it should be roughly 23 x 35 cm (9 x 14 in). Sprinkle with a little flour and cut lengthways into 1 cm (½ in) wide strips. Place the pointy tip of the mould at one end of a pastry strip and roll it at an angle to the other end, overlapping the layers slightly. Place it seam-side down on the lined baking tray and repeat with the rest of the strips, or until you have used all the moulds you have available. Brush thoroughly with the beaten egg.

Bake for 25 minutes, or until golden brown.

Remove from the oven and leave to cool for 1 minute, then transfer to a wire rack until cool enough to touch. Remove the horns from the moulds with a gentle twisting motion and leave until completely cool.

To make the filling, whip the cream with the icing sugar to form soft peaks, then mix in the vanilla. Fill a piping bag with the mixture. Place a few cubes of strawberry at the bottom of each pastry horn, then pipe in some whipped cream until filled to the top. Dust with icing sugar and serve with the strawberry slices alongside.

Chapter 5

Crêpes, Dumplings, Noodles and Grains

There is a long tradition of serving crêpes for dessert in Romania, and almost every restaurant will have them on the menu. They are usually filled with a fruit confiture, rolled like a cigar and dusted with icing (confectioner's) sugar. I also remember Crêpes Suzette, a little moment of glamour since they were flambéed at the table in restaurants. I have included a recipe that takes inspiration from them with the option of no alcohol (on page 140), so you won't run the risk of burning off your eyebrows. In the Banat region, which used to have a large community of German-Swabians, people also make Șmoră (page 130), a shredded pancake with its own distinct ingredients.

Another speciality in Romania are sweet dumplings made with potato dough or semolina, which are first simmered, then rolled in buttery, crunchy breadcrumbs. Many of these dishes are shared with all the other countries and regions that once were under the Habsburg Empire and have German origins. In Romania, plum dumplings are a seasonal recipe in the autumn (fall), although in winter we make them with jam or prunes if needed (see Găluște on page 128).

There are a few desserts prepared with noodles, which are of Jewish influence, and we have a spectacular one in Transylvania: a noodle pudding made with curd cheese and raisins, enveloped in a thin layer of filo pastry, called Vargabéles in Hungarian (see page 133). When made without the filo, it is a Lokshen Kugel in Yiddish and Budincă de macaroane in Romanian. It sounds intriguing and it is wonderful in both versions.

Across the Carpathian mountains to the east, we find dumplings filled with sour cherries, Colțunași (page 143), little triangles of simmered noodles, served hot and accompanied by fruit sauce or a spoonful of sour cream.

Since noodles are made with wheat flour, which is also a sacred symbol of resurrection, they often take on a more ritualistic role in religious celebrations. The recipe for Mucenici muntenești (page 126) calls for the noodles to be simmered with walnuts, honey and vanilla. The same happens with grains in a dish called colivă, where pearl barley or wheat are cooked with nuts and dried fruit. Rice puddings are ubiquitous, dusted with cinnamon or layered with fruit then baked in the oven and served with șodou, vanilla sauce.

This is a chapter of utter comfort and I hope it will delight and excite you.

Crêpes, Dumplings, Noodles and Grains

Apricot Rice Pudding with Wine Sauce

Budincă de orez cu caise și șodou

There is a region in Romania that has a long tradition of growing rice. Rice paddies were established in a marshy part of the Banat region, western Romania, in the 18th century. Italians came here at the invitation of the Habsburg Empire to establish and manage rice fields, building ingenious irrigation systems, some of which are still functioning today. This recipe is a variation on the classic rice pudding, which is very popular in Romania, considered by many of us to be the dessert of our childhoods. Here, I accompany it with a vanilla sauce and the dish is served chilled, proving that rice puddings are not just for autumn (fall) and winter seasons.

Serves 4

50 g (2 oz) unsalted butter
150 g (5 oz/generous ⅔ cup) arborio rice
500 ml (17 fl oz/2 cups) full-fat milk, or as needed
200 ml (7 fl oz/scant 1 cup) double (heavy) cream
80 g (3 oz/⅓ cup) golden caster (superfine) sugar
1 tablespoon orange blossom water
1 teaspoon almond extract
zest of 1 lemon

For the sauce

1 small/medium egg (about 80 g/3 oz)
40 g (1½ oz/3½ tablespoons) golden caster (superfine) sugar
40 ml (2½ tablespoons) sweet white wine or Romanian *Tămâioasă*

For the topping

4 ripe apricots, sliced (fresh or canned)

Heat the butter in a large pan over a medium-low heat until frothy, then add the rice and cook for 3 minutes, stirring often to avoid browning. Add the milk, cream and sugar, and cook until the milk is absorbed and the rice is soft, adding a little extra milk, if needed. Stir in the orange blossom water, almond extract and lemon zest and remove from the heat.

Meanwhile, make the sauce. Beat all the ingredients together in a heatproof bowl, then set it on top of a pan filled with simmering water. Whisk continuously until it thickens, which can happen very quickly. Set aside until ready to serve. You can also chill it, in which case the sauce needs to be whisked briefly before serving.

To serve, place 3 large spoonfuls of rice pudding into each bowl, add a few apricot slices and pour some of the sauce around it.

Notes

For a non-alcoholic version, replace the wine with orange juice, adding 1 teaspoon of almond extract.

If the fruit is not ripe, you can roast it for 15 minutes at 180°C (non-fan)/350°F/gas 4, drizzled with 1 tablespoon of honey.

The pudding is equally delicious without the sauce or roasted fruit, if you don't have time, in which case I serve it dusted with cinnamon.

Pearl Barley Pudding with Dried Fruit

Budincă de arpacaș

Dried fruit, wheat, grains, honey and walnuts are often part of sacred, religious dishes. This fragrant pudding, called *colivă*, is shared as alms in church and often small quantities are left in little pots on gravestones to nourish the souls of those who have departed. It is rather delicious and many people eat it outside of this custom. Restaurants have put it on their menus and some chefs even make ice cream with its flavours.

Serves 4

200 g (7 oz/scant 1 cup) pearl
  barley or cracked wheat
100 g (3½ oz/1 cup) walnuts
80 g (3 oz/⅔ cup) golden
  raisins (sultanas)
4 tablespoons honey
zest and juice of
  1 medium lemon
2 teaspoons ground cinnamon
1½ tablespoons rum (optional)
1–3 tablespoons oat milk
  or other non-dairy milk,
  if needed

To serve

2 teaspoons ground cinnamon
20 g (¾ oz/¼ cup)
  walnuts, chopped

Put the pearl barley in a pan and add enough water to cover. Bring to the boil, then reduce the heat and simmer until the pearl barley is soft, about 20 minutes. Drain in a sieve (strainer), then measure out 80 g (3 oz) and set it aside.

Add the rest of the pearl barley to a food processor together with the remaining ingredients and blitz until the mixture has a thick consistency but is not dry. You might need to add a little non-dairy milk. Taste and adjust the sweetness or the level of rum, if using.

Transfer to a bowl and combine with the reserved pearl barley.

Serve in bowls, dusted with cinnamon and decorate with a few chopped walnuts.

Noodles in Walnut and Vanilla Soup

Mucenici muntenești

These noodles are the southern variation of the baked brioche buns on page 80. The difference is in the ingredients, which are only flour and water, and in the preparation, being simmered in a honey and walnut soup rather than baked. Otherwise, the shape is the same, a looped figure 8, symbolising resurrection, marking the transition from winter to spring and the turning of the seasons. The legend goes that the *Mucenici* were a group of 40 people who were sentenced to death by a Roman legion for their Christian beliefs. However, on the day of their execution, they didn't die. While this miracle in itself convinced some Roman soldiers to convert to the new religion, the sentence was still carried out. Eventually, the victims were recognised as martyrs and they have been celebrated ever since.

Serves 4

For the dough

90 ml (3 fl oz/⅓ cup) hot water
150 g (5 oz/1¼ cups) plain (all-purpose) flour, plus extra for dusting
1 pinch of salt

For the soup

700 ml (24 fl oz/scant 3 cups) water
50 g (2 oz/¼ cup) golden caster (superfine) sugar
1½ tablespoons honey
125 g (4 oz/1 cup) walnuts, coarsely crushed, plus extra to serve
zest of 2 lemons, plus extra to serve
2 teaspoons vanilla bean paste
2 teaspoons vanilla extract
2 teaspoons ground cinnamon, plus extra to serve
3 tablespoons rum (optional)

Start one day ahead. Mix all the ingredients for the dough in a bowl and knead for a few minutes. Cover and leave to rest for 15 minutes, then knead again and rest for a further 15 minutes.

Heat the oven to its lowest temperature.

Divide the dough into 7–8 g (¼ oz) balls, then roll each into an 8 cm (3 in) rope, bring the ends together into a circle, and twist in the middle to form the shape of the number 8. Place on a generously floured baking sheet. When you finish them all, toss them in the flour and place in the oven for 2 hours. The aim here is to dry them out. Leave to cool overnight in a dry room.

The next day, bring the water to the boil with the sugar and honey. Add the *mucenici* noodles and simmer for 20 minutes. Add the crushed walnuts and lemon zest, and cook for a further 10 minutes. Remove from the heat and add the vanillas, cinnamon and rum, if using.

Serve warm with more chopped walnuts, lemon zest and cinnamon on the side for people to adjust the flavours to their preference.

Damson Dumplings with Buttery Breadcrumbs

Găluște cu prune

These dumplings are a seasonal dessert in Romania, usually made in the autumn (fall) when local plums are at their best. Variations of these dumplings are dotted across all the countries that were once under the Habsburg Empire, and therefore became popular in those regions of Romania that were under direct Austrian rule. Today, they are eaten throughout the country. When plums are not in season, people use jam or prunes, and here in the UK I love to use damsons.

Makes 16

500 g (1 lb 2 oz) potatoes, diced
1 tablespoon sunflower oil
1 medium egg, beaten
130 g (4 oz/1 cup) plain (all-purpose) flour, plus extra for dusting
16 small damsons or plums, cut in half and pitted

For the coating

40 g (1½ oz/3 tablespoons) unsalted butter
150 g (5 oz/2 cups) dried breadcrumbs
80 g (3 oz/⅓ cup) caster (superfine) or golden caster sugar
1 pinch of salt
2 teaspoons ground cinnamon

In a large pan, boil the potatoes until soft. Drain and return them to the pan over a low heat to evaporate as much water as possible. Add the oil and mash them with a fork. Set aside to cool completely.

Meanwhile, prepare the breadcrumbs by heating the butter in a large frying pan (skillet). When it reaches a deep golden colour, add the breadcrumbs and cook for 10 minutes, stirring often. Be careful, as they can burn very quickly. Remove from the heat and allow to cool, then stir in the sugar, salt and cinnamon. Spread the mixture over a shallow plate.

When the potatoes have cooled, add the egg and flour, and knead briefly by hand. It will be a rather soft, sticky dough, but this is what makes the dumplings light and fluffy.

Flour your workspace and your hands generously, and gently roll the dough into a log, 50 cm (20 in) long. Divide it into 16 pieces. Keep flouring your palms and fingers lightly. Take one piece of dough and press it into a circle in your palm. Stick together two plum halves and place them in the middle of the disc, seal the dough around them well, then roll it between your palms. Place on a baking sheet and repeat with the rest.

Bring a large pan of water to the boil, then add the dumplings in batches and simmer for up to 10 minutes. They should rise to the surface of the water when ready. Use a slotted spoon to take them out, then roll them gently in the breadcrumbs.

Arrange on a large plate and serve.

Shredded Semolina Pancakes with Strawberries

Șmoră cu griș

This thick, rich pancake is specific to the Banat region in western Romania. The recipe was given to me by Halrun Reinholz, from a Swabian family in Timișoara, the capital of Banat. Halrun makes it with yoghurt and semolina, and serves it with plum compote, and she says that jam or any other fresh fruit work well too. In her husband's family, they have a recipe where the shredded pancakes are sprinkled with sugar and topped with a salad of cucumbers, dill and garlic. It is one of their favourite family dishes. While I would have liked to share the recipe here, it is more on the savoury side than sweet, therefore I shall tempt you instead with a semolina *șmoră* with fresh fruit.

Serves 4

2 tablespoons unsalted butter
400 g (14 oz) fresh
  strawberries, sliced and
  lightly mashed

For the batter

300 g (10½ oz/1¼ cups) thick,
  plain yoghurt
3 medium eggs, separated
3 tablespoons golden caster
  (superfine) sugar, plus extra
  to serve
120 g (4 oz/1 cup)
  wheat semolina
½ teaspoon baking powder
zest of 1 lemon

First, make the batter. In a bowl, mix the yoghurt with the egg yolks and sugar. Add the semolina gradually, stirring constantly, followed by the baking powder and lemon zest. Beat the egg whites in a separate bowl and fold into the batter.

Heat the butter in a 25 cm (10 in) frying pan (skillet) over a medium heat. Pour in all of the batter and cook for 3–4 minutes until nicely golden underneath. Use a rubber spatula to divide the pancake into quarters, turn the pieces and cook for a further 3–4 minutes.

Shred the pancakes into smaller pieces and divide among 4 serving plates. Top with the lightly mashed strawberries and sprinkle with caster sugar.

Noodle Pudding with Curd Cheese

Budincă de tăiţei cu brânză Vargabéles

This is a magnificent pudding from Transylvania. The *fideo* noodles or vermicelli pasta are simmered and tossed with sweet curd cheese and raisins, flavoured generously with vanilla and wrapped in thin filo pastry. It goes in the oven at a low temperature to form a beautifully golden crust, while the middle stays soft and delicious. It is a pudding with Jewish ancestry and only in Hungarian communities in Transylvania is it made with filo and called *Vargabéles*. In the rest of the country, it is prepared without filo and goes by the name of *budincă de tăiţei*. I chose to follow the Transylvanian tradition, since it is unusual and surprisingly delightful in texture, but feel free to omit the pastry if you like.

Makes 8 generous slices

250 g (9 oz) vermicelli pasta or *tăiţei* (see page 134) or tagliatelle
250 g (9 oz/generous 1 cup) curd cheese or ricotta
100 g (3½ oz/scant ½ cup) sour cream
2 tablespoons fine semolina
2 medium eggs, separated
100 g (3½ oz/scant ½ cup) golden caster (superfine) sugar
120 g (4 oz/1 cup) golden raisins (sultanas)
2 teaspoons vanilla bean paste
3 tablespoons unsalted butter, melted
6 sheets filo pastry
icing (confectioner's) sugar, for dusting

Preheat the oven to 160°C (non-fan)/320°F/gas 2.

To make the filling, mix the curd cheese in a bowl with the sour cream, semolina, egg yolks, sugar, golden raisins and vanilla. In a separate bowl, whisk the egg whites to stiff peaks, then fold into the cheese mixture.

In a large pan, bring enough water to cover the pasta to the boil. Cook the vermicelli, if using, for 2 minutes or the pasta for 5–8 minutes, then drain.

Combine the pasta with the cheese filling.

Brush a 20 x 30 x 6 cm (8 x 12 x 2½ in) baking tray (pan) with a little melted butter. Place 3 filo sheets on the base of the tray, brushing with butter between each layer. Trim the filo sheets to the size of the tray. Spread the pasta mixture evenly on top, then cover with the remaining 3 filo sheets, brushing each with butter as before. Brush the top with the remaining melted butter.

Bake for 40 minutes, then remove from the oven and cover with a clean dish towel. This will soften the layers and make it easy to slice.

Serve at room temperature, dusted with icing sugar. It is equally delicious cold, the following day.

Crêpes, Dumplings, Noodles and Grains

Noodles with Poppy Seeds

Iofcă cu mac

This is a dish that my grandfather used to cook for me, when he wanted to spoil me. It is very easy to make, and the textures of noodles and poppy seeds combined are intriguing. In some parts of the country, they are made with poppy seeds. *Iofca* noodles take their name from the Turkish *yufka*, which is a thin dough baked into a flatbread. The noodles are traditionally cut into wide strips, squares or diamond shapes, and I added a little wholemeal flour to enhance the nutty flavour. It works just as well with store-bought pasta, including wholemeal pasta, but you will miss the subtle flavours of making it from scratch.

Serves 2

For the noodles
200 g (7 oz/ 1⅓ cups) plain (all-purpose) flour, plus extra for dusting
2 medium eggs
2 tablespoons water
1 pinch of salt, plus extra for the pasta water

For the topping
125 g (4 oz/generous ¾ cup) poppy seeds
50 g (2 oz/¼ cup) golden caster (superfine) sugar

To finish
1½ tablespoons unsalted butter

Make the noodle dough by mixing together all the ingredients in a bowl. Add another ½ tablespoon of water, if the dough looks too dry. Knead for 5 minutes, then cover and leave to rest for 15 minutes. Knead again for 5 minutes, then rest for a further 15 minutes.

Lightly dust the work surface with flour and roll out the dough as thinly as possible, to 40-50 cm (16-20 in) in diameter.

Cut the dough into 5 cm (2 in) wide strips, then cut diagonally across the strips at 4cm (1½ in) intervals to create diamond shapes.

Bring a large pan of water to the boil, add a pinch of salt and simmer the *iofca* noodles until cooked through but still firm, about 8 minutes.

Heat the butter in a frying pan (skillet) until melted, then add the noodles and toss briefly, adding the poppy seeds and sugar topping at the end. Toss again just a few times, then serve immediately as the sugar needs to stay crunchy.

Simmered Curd Cheese and Semolina Dumplings with Bilberry Jam

Papanași fierți

The country is divided over these dumplings: some of us know them as fried doughnuts, while others as simmered dumplings. It's rather a city vs countryside divide, or restaurant vs home cooking. Here, I go back to a traditional recipe, which was prepared for me by the team at Mihai Eminescu Trust, the first organisation to begin restoring the old way of Saxon life in Transylvania and to inspire the philosophy of the self-sustained village. The dish is considered to be of German origin and is enjoyed throughout the country.

Serves 4

For the coating

30 g (1 oz) unsalted butter
120 g (4 oz/1½ cups) very fine dried breadcrumbs
50 g (2 oz/¼ cup) caster (superfine) sugar
2 teaspoons ground cinnamon

For the dumplings

300 g (10½ oz/1⅓ cups) Romanian *brânză de vaci* or plain full-fat cream cheese
1 medium egg
100 g (3½ oz/generous ¾ cup) fine semolina
30 g (1 oz/¼ cup) plain (all-purpose) flour
1 pinch of salt

To serve

200 g (7 oz/⅔ cup) bilberry jam (or blackcurrant, blueberry or strawberry)

First, prepare the coating. Melt the butter in a large frying pan (skillet) over a medium heat until it smells slightly toasted. Stir in the breadcrumbs, turn the heat to low if the pan seems too hot, and keep stirring gently for 5–8 minutes until they turn a light golden colour. Remove from the heat and stir in the sugar and cinnamon. Set aside.

Prepare the dumplings by combining all the ingredients, except the salt, in a bowl. The mixture should fall off the spoon and have the consistency of very thick double (heavy) cream.

Bring a pan of water to the boil with a pinch of salt, then reduce the heat to medium. Using a teaspoon, place some of the dumpling mixture in the water. Work in small batches. Simmer for 6–7 minutes until soft but still a little firm.

Use a slotted spoon to transfer them from the water straight into the pan with the breadcrumbs, shaking the pan so the dumplings get a golden coating on all sides.

Serve them warm or cold with your favourite jam.

Crêpes with Toffee Apple and Rosemary Sauce

Clătite cu sos de mere și rozmarin

In Romania, our tables are graced by a wealth of recipes using crêpes, ranging from the easiest ones, filled with confiture and rolled like a cigar, to more elaborate dishes that can be baked and topped with meringue. I also remember Crêpes Suzette, a popular dish on restaurant menus in the 1980s. Flambéed at the table, it was a rare occasion to enjoy the spectacle of silver service available to 'the working people of the Socialist Republic of Romania'. The recipe below will not ask you to light anything on fire, even though it uses a small amount of alcohol. It also celebrates a wonderful, much-loved fruit in Romania: apple, invigorated here by the herby spiciness of a few sprigs of rosemary.

Makes 8

unsalted butter, for frying

For the crêpes

2 medium eggs
100 g (3½ oz/generous ¾ cup)
   plain (all-purpose) flour
1 teaspoon golden caster
   (superfine) sugar
1 pinch of salt
220 ml (8 fl oz/scant 1 cup)
   full-fat milk

For the sauce

30 g (1 oz/2 tablespoons)
   golden caster (superfine)
   sugar
200 ml (7 fl oz/scant 1 cup)
   apple juice
3 tablespoons lime juice
   (from 1–2 limes)
1 tablespoon verjuice or apple
   cider vinegar
3 rosemary sprigs
   (each 8–10 cm/4 in long)
2 tablespoons Calvados
   or fruit brandy (optional)
40 g (1½ oz) unsalted butter

To serve (optional)

orange marmalade or any
   of your favourite jams

Make the crêpes by mixing the eggs with the flour, sugar and salt in a bowl. Add the milk little by little to make a smooth batter, then place the bowl in the refrigerator for 30 minutes.

Heat ½ teaspoon of butter in a frying pan (skillet) over a medium heat. Using a ladle, pour in enough batter to thinly and evenly coat the base of the pan, tilting the pan to move the mixture around. Leave to cook for about 30 seconds until golden underneath, then ease a palette knife under the crêpe to lift and flip it over. Add a knob of butter each time you flip, if you like. Cook for a further 30 seconds, then transfer to a plate. Repeat with the remaining batter, adding butter as needed.

You can use the same pan to make the sauce, just wipe away any remaining butter. Melt the sugar in the pan over a medium heat until caramelised. You may need to tilt the pan every now and then to make sure that it melts evenly without burning. When it turns dark golden, remove from the heat and add the apple juice, lime juice and verjuice together with the rosemary sprigs. Return the pan to the heat and simmer until the caramel has dissolved, about 3–5 minutes. Stir in the Calvados (if using) and butter, then simmer until slightly reduced and thickened, 5–8 minutes.

Spread the crêpes with a little marmalade, if using, and fold in four. Place on a serving dish deep enough to hold the toffee apple sauce. Pour the hot sauce on top and serve immediately.

Dumplings with Sour Cherries

Colțunași cu vișine

These are especially popular in the eastern part of Romania, in Moldavia. Traditionally filled either with sweet curd cheese or fruit, they are served with crème fraîche or fruit sauce. Sour cherries make for a very special appearance since the season is so short, and they are very treasured. *Colțunași* are a relative of Polish *pierogi* and Russian *vareniki*, and in Romania they have the distinctive triangular shape that also gives them the name. They are served right away and if you need to simmer them in batches, toss them all in butter in a warm pan before serving.

Serves 4

For the dough
300 g (10½ oz/scant 2½ cups) plain (all-purpose) flour, plus extra for dusting
1 medium egg
2 tablespoons sunflower oil
100 ml (3½ fl oz/scant ½ cup) water

For the sauce
200 g (7 oz) sour cherries (or any soft fruit)
50 g (2 oz/¼ cup) golden caster (superfine) sugar

For the filling
200 g (7 oz) sour cherries (or small cherries, or any soft fruit), roughly chopped if large

Make the dough by mixing all the ingredients in a bowl, then knead until it looks smooth and shiny, and is not sticky. Cover and leave to rest for 15 minutes. Knead again briefly, then rest for a further 15 minutes at room temperature. Before rolling and shaping, knead again a few times. This process will develop the elasticity of the dough. You can leave it in the refrigerator overnight, if you wish, but bring it back to room temperature before rolling.

Meanwhile, make the sauce. In a small pan, lightly stew the sour cherries with the sugar until the sugar is dissolved. Press with a fork to mash everything together, then set aside. You can make this a day ahead, if you wish.

Lightly flour the work surface and a baking sheet. Divide the dough in half and roll out one half with a rolling pin or using a pasta machine as thinly as you can. Cut into 8 cm (3 in) squares. Place 2–3 pieces of fresh sour cherries (depending on their size) in each square, then fold into triangles to enclose the cherries. You might need to brush one side of the dough with a little water so it seals properly. Place on the baking sheet, while you repeat with the remaining dough.

Bring one or two pans of water to the boil, add the dumplings and simmer for 5 minutes. Serve immediately with the fruit sauce on the side.

Chapter 6

Doughnuts and Fritters

Doughnuts and fritters are very much the realm of home cooks, comfort food for when we don't want to bake a cake or use the oven. We love doughnuts in Romania in a multitude of shapes and fillings, from a very quick recipe based on a yoghurt batter and fried choux pastry, to German-style Berliner doughnuts, or a flatbread style made with potato.

Langoși demonstrate the latter type very well. They are deep-fried flatbreads, quite large, topped with sour cream and cheese or – in their sweet version – with jam. Popular mostly in Transylvania, being of Hungarian origin, they are an iconic street food staple and popular festival fare. The recipe on page 166 also offers a glimpse into the Hungarian communities here, including the story of the first cookery book printed for the public in Transylvania.

Traditionally, before oil became so popular, doughnuts and fritters would have been fried in lard, or had lard among the ingredients. Today, a typical dough contains flour, eggs, dairy and fat, whether butter or oil, and they are yeasted. The quick versions are more like a batter and use bicarbonate of soda (baking soda) or baking powder for leavening, which reacts instantly with the hot oil and makes very fluffy doughnuts.

This is a chapter full of warmth and delicious happiness, and I hope it will bring as much joy to your table as it brings us in Romania.

Doughnuts and Fritters

Quick Doughnuts with Cinnamon Sugar

Gogoși rapide cu scorțișoară

This recipe is delightful in its simplicity and aroma. It comes together so quickly that you really need to be ready to eat the doughnuts before you start to cook. The cinnamon-sugar combination is very warming.

Serves 4–6

vegetable oil, for deep-frying

For the batter

200 g (7 oz/generous ¾ cup) thick, full-fat yoghurt
1 medium egg
55 g (2 oz/¼ cup) caster (superfine) sugar
150 g (5 oz/1¼ cups) plain (all-purpose) flour
zest of 2 lemons
½ teaspoon almond extract
½ teaspoon baking powder

For dusting

50 g (2 oz/scant ½ cup) icing (confectioner's) sugar
2 teaspoons ground cinnamon

Set a small deep pan over a high heat and pour in enough oil for the doughnuts to be half-submerged.

In a bowl, whisk the yoghurt with the egg and sugar, then add the rest of the batter ingredients. The consistency of the batter should be very thick.

Mix the icing sugar and ground cinnamon for dusting on a shallow plate and set aside.

When the oil is hot (about 170°C/338°F), reduce the heat to medium. Take ½ tablespoon of the batter and slide it into the oil. Be careful not to splash. Work in batches of 3–4 doughnuts at a time and ensure that the temperature of the oil stays constant. Cook for just a few minutes until golden brown, constantly turning them with a slotted spoon so they cook on both sides. Remove from the pan and immediately roll in the cinnamon sugar.

Allow the doughnuts to cool, then serve.

Pastry Fritters with a Vanilla Glaze

Minciunele cu zahăr vanilat

An old-time favourite family recipe, these fritters are ready very quickly, as they don't use any yeast. They are usually rolled in vanilla icing (confectioner's) sugar, but I have used an unorthodox thin vanilla glaze in this recipe. Feel free to use either, since they will not become too sweet.

Makes about 30

180 g (6½ oz/generous ¾ cup) sour cream
1 large egg
2 teaspoons vanilla bean paste
40 g (1¾ oz/3½ tablespoons) golden caster (superfine) sugar
¼ teaspoon bicarbonate of soda (baking soda)
400 g (14 oz/3¼ cups) plain (all-purpose) flour, plus extra for dusting

For the glaze

3 tablespoons icing (confectioner's) sugar
3 tablespoons warm milk
1 teaspoon vanilla extract
1 tablespoon rum (optional)

For frying

250 ml (8½ fl oz/1 cup) sunflower oil

In a bowl, mix the sour cream with the egg and vanilla, then add the sugar, bicarbonate of soda and flour, and knead for 10 minutes. Cover the bowl and place in the refrigerator for 20 minutes.

Make the glaze by mixing all the ingredients in a small bowl, then set aside.

Heat the oil for frying in a small frying pan (skillet), you will work in batches.

Divide the dough in half. Roll out one half to a rectangle or square, 3 mm (⅛ in) thick. Cut into strips, 4 cm (1½ in) wide, then cut each strip on an angle into 8 cm (3 in) pieces, so they resemble diamonds. Sprinkle the tops with a little flour. Make a small slit widthways in the middle of each diamond, then pull one of the pointed ends through it, making a little twist. Place on a floured baking sheet and repeat with the other half of the dough.

Carefully place a few of the twists at a time into the hot oil. Fry for 1 minute on one side, then turn with a slotted spoon until golden brown on both sides. You may need to adjust the heat, turning it up or down to avoid burning the doughnuts. Use a slotted spoon to remove them to kitchen paper to drain.

Brush with the glaze while still warm.

You can eat them as you go along or allow to cool before serving.

Pastry Fritters with Rosewater Syrup

Gogoși împinse

This recipe has a royal glow. It first appeared in the 16th-century *The Cookbook of the Chef to the Transylvanian Royal Court*, where a whole chapter was dedicated to doughnuts. I found it mentioned by historian Lukács József in 2019, who explained the method in detail. The mixture was first boiled, then mixed with eggs and 'pushed' through a wooden tube with a star nozzle at the end, possibly similar to a sausage-filling machine. The little doughnuts were fried in lard or butter, then sprinkled with sugar. They are similar to the Spanish *churros*, to which they are no doubt related through the Arabic influence that is visible today in many cuisines in Europe and the Balkans. In parts of southern Romania and in neighbouring Bulgaria, they are called *tulumbe* and are soaked in syrup, and this is the way I prepare them in this recipe.

Serves 4

For the batter

180 ml (6 fl oz/¾ cup)
   full-fat milk
45 g (1¾ oz) unsalted butter
100 g (3½ oz/generous ¾ cup)
   plain (all-purpose) flour
3 medium eggs

For the syrup

25 g (¾ oz/2 tablespoons)
   caster (superfine) sugar
25 g (¾ oz/1½ tablespoons)
   honey
25 ml (scant 2 tablespoons)
   water
1 tablespoon lemon juice
1 tablespoon rosewater

For frying

100 ml (3½ oz/scant ½ cup)
   vegetable oil

In a pan, bring the milk and butter to the boil. Sift in the flour and whisk vigorously until it comes away from the sides of the pan and looks shiny. Remove from the heat and use a wooden spoon to quickly stir in the eggs, one by one. The batter should be thick, barely falling off the spoon, but easy to pipe. Spoon the batter into a piping bag fitted with a medium (1 cm/½ in) star nozzle.

Make the syrup by bringing the sugar, honey, water and lemon juice to the boil in a small pan. Reduce the heat and simmer for 10 minutes until it thickens slightly. Add the rosewater and allow to cool.

Heat the oil in a medium deep pan to 170°C (338°F).

Pipe the batter into the hot oil, holding the bag with one hand and a pair of scissors in the other, cutting the pastry into 6–8 cm (2¼–3¼ in) lengths. Don't overcrowd the pan and work in batches. Use a slotted spoon to turn the fritters, making sure they cook evenly for 3–4 minutes. Remove to kitchen paper to drain.

Arrange the hot fritters on a plate and either drizzle the syrup on top or soak them briefly in the syrup before serving. Serve immediately or as you fry them.

Doughnuts with Zesty Curd Cheese

Gogoși ardeleneşti cu urdă

Depending on where you are in the country, these doughnuts are known under different names and come in different sizes. In Transylvania and the Banat region, they are *gogoși* or *crofne*, and sometimes can even reach the size of a small plate. Their distinct feature comes from the golden ring around the middle, while the filling can be either jam or curd cheese, *urdă*, mixed with egg yolks and sweetened with sugar. Although slightly adapted, the recipe below was sent by Liliana Coșorean from the small Saxon village of Florești, and skilfully prepared for me by her good friend Denisa Babeș in Mălâncrav, as they both have them on the menus at their guesthouses.

Makes 12

300 g (10½ oz/scant 2½ cups) plain (all-pupose) flour, plus extra for dusting

10 g (1½ sachets) fast-action dried yeast

30 g (1 oz/3 tablespoons) golden caster (superfine) sugar

1 pinch of salt

160 ml (5½ fl oz/⅔ cup) full-fat milk, warm

2 medium egg yolks

25 g (¾ oz/1¾ tablespoons) unsalted butter, very soft but not melted

400 ml (13 fl oz/generous 1½ cups) vegetable oil, plus extra for greasing

icing (confectioner's) sugar, for dusting

For the filling

200 g (7 oz/scant 1 cup) curd cheese or ricotta

50 g (2 oz/¼ cup) golden caster (superfine) sugar

zest of 1 lemon

1 egg yolk (optional, as it will be raw)

In a bowl, mix together the flour, yeast, sugar, salt and milk, then add the egg yolks and mix well. Add the butter in two stages, incorporating after each addition. Transfer the dough to a lightly oiled bowl, cover and leave to prove in a warm place for 1½ hours.

Flour the work surface generously and turn the dough onto it. Gently press and stretch the dough out to 8–10 mm (⅓–½ in) thick; use a rolling pin if you wish to be accurate, but press ever so slightly on it. Move the dough once or twice to make sure it is not sticking to the surface. Use a 9 cm (3½ in) round cookie cutter to cut out rounds, then cover with a clean cloth and leave to prove on the work surface for 40 minutes.

Heat the oil in a small, deep pan with a lid to 165–170°C (329–338°F). When hot, slide in 2 doughnuts with the floured sides facing up. Cover the pan with the lid and fry for a few seconds until they have puffed up. Use a slotted spoon to turn them over and cook for a few seconds without the lid. By now, they should have formed a white ring around the middle. Transfer to kitchen paper to drain, then dust with icing sugar while they are still warm. Repeat to cook the rest of the doughnuts.

To make the filling, whisk all the ingredients together in a bowl until well combined.

In my experience, not all doughnuts will expand to the same size, so enjoy them whatever the shape. Traditionally, they are filled by poking a hole in the white ring with the handle of a wooden spoon. You can use a piping bag to fill them, but I prefer to keep them intact and serve the filling as a dip or spread.

Fruit Medley Fritters with Tarragon Honey Drizzle

Mere și alte fructe în pijama

This ridiculously easy dessert is usually made with apples, but other fruit work surprisingly well too. Try them with apricots and peaches, or with other tangy fruit. I use honey to drizzle on top and to add sweetness, as there is no sugar in the batter. Here I chose to infuse it with herbs, tarragon being my favourite when it comes to pairing herbs with fruit.

Serves 4

100 g (3½ oz/generous ¾ cup)
   plain (all-purpose) flour
150 ml (5 fl oz/scant ⅔ cup)
   full-fat milk
1 medium egg
2 apples
juice of ½ lemon
2 peaches
2 apricots
vegetable oil, for deep-frying

For the drizzle

3 tablespoons honey
1 teaspoon chopped
   fresh tarragon

Put the flour in a bowl and gradually pour in the milk, mixing well to avoid any lumps forming. Add the egg and combine well. Place in the refrigerator while you are preparing the fruit.

Cut the apples into round slices, then remove the cores with a small cookie cutter or knife. Place in a bowl and drizzle with the lemon juice. Slice the peaches and apricots, avoiding the pits.

For the drizzle, mix the honey and tarragon in a small bowl and set aside.

Heat enough oil for deep-frying in a small pan. Dip a few slices of fruit in the batter, then fry in the hot oil for a couple of minutes. Remove with a slotted spoon to drain on kitchen paper. Work in batches and repeat with the remaining fruit.

Drizzle with the tarragon honey and serve immediately.

Courgette Fritters with Caster Sugar

Chiftelute de dovlecei

This is what happens when Romanians use their imaginations when cooking seasonal ingredients, especially those growing in abundance. Courgettes (zucchini) are a prolific crop and cooks may find themselves at a loss as to what to do with them. These fritters are soft, almost like a thick pancake, while the much-needed texture comes from the caster (superfine) sugar sprinkled on top.

Serves 4

300 g (10½ oz) courgette (zucchini), grated
2½ teaspoons caster (superfine) sugar, plus at least 4 teaspoons, to serve
2 medium eggs
80 g (3 oz/⅔ cup) plain (all-purpose) flour
zest of 1 lemon
1 pinch of salt
150 ml (5 fl oz/scant ⅔ cup) sunflower oil, for frying

In a bowl, combine the grated courgettes with the 2½ teaspoons of sugar and leave to macerate for 10 minutes. Squeeze as much water as possible out of the courgettes, then place them in a bowl and mix with the eggs, flour, lemon zest and salt.

Heat the oil in a medium frying pan (skillet) over a medium–high heat, adjusting the heat as you go along to keep the temperature of the oil constant. Place spoonfuls of the batter in the oil, and flatten them slightly. Cook for a few minutes on each side to a rich golden colour. Remove with a slotted spoon to drain on kitchen paper.

Sprinkle the hot fritters with the 4 teaspoons of caster sugar and serve immediately.

GOGOȘI
CU BRÂNZĂ DE BURDUF
Conține: făină, zer/abur, zahăr, drojdie, sâe, branza de burduf

PREȚ 5.00 lei /100 gr.

Magyars in Transylvania

✕ ✕ ✕ ✕ ✕ ✕ ✕ ✕ ✕ ✕ ✕ ✕ ✕ ✕ ✕ ✕ ✕ ✕ ✕

'This little book does not hasten to help those chefs who work at royal courts and who know by heart how to cook dishes with great taste, but comes to the rescue of those hard working people with honest kitchens who often don't have their own cook. However, it can be used by people of all ranks. So dear reader, if you find that you like this little book, use it and stay in good health.' So wrote the author of the first cookery book published in 1695 in Transylvania, *Cărticica meseriei de bucătar*, (*The Cook's Booklet*). It was printed in Hungarian and was the first of its kind available to the public. As often was the case in those times, it had an anonymous author; the cover only bore the name of the Master Printer and his publishing house.

After much speculation and debate as to whether the author was a protestant or catholic Hungarian, or perhaps even a Franciscan monk due to the growing influence of monastic education at the time, historian Lukács József brings the answer to light. He writes in the preface of the Romanian translation in 2019 that indeed the author was a protestant and, even better, a woman. Sofia Tofeus was the daughter of a high dignitary at the Royal Court of Transylvania, and the person who almost certainly put the recipes together. This also made her the first published female author of a cookery book at the time in Hungarian Transylvania. Sofia would have grown up in a house with a vast collection of books, her father being an author himself, and would have often accompanied her family at the court as a guest. Therefore, she was as familiar with the kind of dishes that were served at official dinners as the ones prepared at home by her father's cooks.

In cities, the cooks of sweet foods looked to Vienna for ideas of puddings and biscuits, while also drawing inspiration from the region's Turkish occupation with their pastries and confections. Filo dough was used for strudels, fried breads for *langoşi* and *dulceață lictar* for fruit conserves. Doughnuts seem to have been very popular at the time, alongside honey breads and lard biscuits. In time, coffee became a popular drink whether in coffee houses or at home at the end of a meal.

Sofia Tofeus gathered her collection of recipes to help people 'of all ranks' and found a family friend, no other than Miklós Misztótfalusi Kis, to print it. Kis was already held in high regard by the Hungarian nobility, having made 'a little Netherlands out of Transylvania'. He learnt the skill of printing books in the Netherlands, which was known as the land of printing presses and the bookshop of the world. On his return, he became one of the greatest Hungarian printers.

Lukács József considers this recipe book to have been the culmination of the Transylvanian Renaissance in the kitchen, containing dishes that were known to high society, but were not available in print to everyone. This explains why it was such a success from the beginning.

The book contained an impressive number of jams called *lictar*, and also many recipes for doughnuts (including one that was 'pushed'), breads sweetened with both honey and sugar, and bread puddings – one of which caught my attention: Old Woman's Doughnut, a pudding made with a sort of *pain perdu*. Light sponge biscuits, *biscotum*, and fruits served fresh but mixed with honey and spices were also listed. Some

Doughnuts and Fritters

recipes were for preparing almond extract and milk, marzipan and fruit syrups.

At the time this cookery book was published, Transylvania was undergoing a significant cultural transformation. The story behind the book showed economic prosperity and a sophisticated cuisine, while the region transitioned from an independent principality under Ottoman control to being subject to the direct rule of the Habsburg Empire. Even though the new Imperial Governor didn't abolish the old political power structures, the Magyar Hungarians felt under the threat of being assimilated. For the next two centuries, they focused on building a national identity, through culture, politics and language, especially by making the most of the power of printed books. This strategy significantly deteriorated the status of other groups, especially peasants, regardless of their ethnicity, with Romanians paying the heaviest toll.

When Transylvania joined Romania in 1918 to form the state we know today, it was a terrible blow for Hungary, having lost other territory to neighbouring countries at the disintegration of the Austro-Hungarian Empire. Parts of the land, formerly in the hands of the Magyar nobility, was now distributed among the peasants. The Second World War and the Communist regime worsened the situation, with many grand properties being nationalised and misused before being left to crumble, while the rightful owners fled the country to save their lives. Glamorous ballrooms and libraries were used as storage for hay or fodder, which damaged them almost beyond repair. After the fall of the communist regime, many of these families came back and at their own expense, or sometimes helped by international funding, restored what was left of their heritage. In a bid to secure their future, some buildings were turned into museums, event venues or restoration projects for students. Remarkable, when you consider all that happened.

There are many Hungarian families living in Romania. I asked Lorant Szocs, who speaks both languages fluently, which of the two countries feels most like home to him. 'We are pretty much a Hungarian family with Hungarian traditions who live in Romania. Transylvania is home and my favourite region, since it reflects all of Romania's culinary richness.' His family story is typical of so many Hungarian families in Romania and speaks of common values. The way Lorant remembers, with great fondness, his grandmothers and their comforting dishes supporting him through the ups and downs of life is no different from how I remember my own.

Lorant tells me about his grandmother Erzsebet, who used to make *hájas tészta*, *haiosi* in Romanian, saying they are the best jam puff pastries in the world, having a unique flakiness. I can believe this, as Lorant works in the UK as Global Senior Development Chef for Jamie Oliver international restaurants and brands. He remembers his grandmother's cakes made with the highly aromatic acacia honey, a characteristicly Romanian honey, and the *rétes tészta*, an exquisite strudel for using up windfall apples. A good, traditional *zserbó*, a layered cake with jam and walnuts, and a *rigo*, a rich chocolate mousse cake, spark memories for him too.

Traditional home baking was carried out mostly by women and I was interested to learn about the dishes of a mixed Romanian-Hungarian family. Was I to find something different here? Through a good friend in Bucharest, I found Rebeka Stamate, now in her eighties, born in Sovata, a spa town with the largest warm-water lake in Europe. From a Hungarian family with many children, Rebeka almost apologetically says that they 'often fried things for dessert', but I know how delicious they must have been. She refers to an abundance of dishes from *langoși*, doughnuts, apples fritters, pancakes topped with apples and meringue, and even chimney cakes, *kürtőskalács* (I owe her the advice on how to bake jam puff pastries!). Born in a Reformed family, she married a Romanian and worked a lifetime in the kitchen of the

Theological Institute in Bucharest. This didn't stop her from giving me a recipe for 'attracting boys', which proved to be a jam cookie baked in an *Işler* style. For feast days, she told me I needed to make *dobos* and *zserbó*, a testimony to how elaborate home baking in our part of the world still is.

These remarkable grandmothers and mothers share a repertoire that is common regardless of family origins. Many cakes and pastries like these are shared by Romanians too and delight many more people outside Transylvania. Cakes and desserts are never thought of as being complicated, and, just like in *The Cook's Booklet*, they can be as much for royalty as for the rest of us.

Hungarian Fried Breads with Stewed Plums and Sour Cream

Langoși cu prune și smântână

Famous in both Transylvania and Hungary, these are a cross between doughnuts and flatbreads (the word *láng* meaning 'flame'). *Langoși* need to have distinct white patches when fried and be at least the size of an 18-cm (7-in) side plate. But they can also be bigger! The traditional toppings are garlic sauce, cheese and crème fraîche, with a sweet version that uses plum jam. The addition of potatoes to the dough is typical of Transylvania, to make the flour go further and also to add softness. Enjoy them warm as soon as they are fried.

Serves 6

325 g (11 oz/generous 2½ cups) plain (all-purpose) flour
150 g (5 oz) mashed potatoes, cold
100 ml (3½ fl oz/scant ½ cup) full-fat milk
1 tablespoon sunflower oil, plus extra for greasing
1 medium egg
4 teaspoons caster (superfine) sugar
7 g (1 sachet) fast-action dried yeast
400 ml (13 fl oz/generous 1½ cups) vegetable oil

For the topping

400 g (14 oz) plums or damsons, halved
40 g (1¾ oz/3½ tablespoons) caster (superfine) sugar
zest and juice of 1 lemon

To serve

150 g (5 oz/⅔ cup) crème fraîche or sour cream

In a bowl, combine the flour and mashed potatoes.

In a separate bowl, mix together the milk, oil, egg, sugar and yeast, then set aside for 5 minutes.

Add the wet ingredients to the dry, then knead for a few minutes until everything is well combined. It is quite a sticky, wet dough. Transfer to a lightly oiled bowl, cover and leave to prove in a warm place for 1 hour.

Make the topping by stewing the fruit in a pan with the sugar until soft, then add the lemon zest and juice. Leave to cool.

Heat the oil in a frying pan (skillet) large enough for the doughnut to fit in. You are going to shape and fry one doughnut at a time.

Transfer the dough onto a well-oiled work surface and divide it into 6 portions. Add more oil to the area where you are shaping the doughnuts, so they don't stick. Gently press with your fingertips to form a round shape, thinner in the middle and thicker around the edges. It should be about 25 cm (10 in) in diameter, or smaller if you don't have a large enough pan.

Lift the dough by the thick edge and carefully place it in the oil, working away from you. Work confidently and quickly and don't worry if the dough loses its shape slightly – it will recover during frying. Cook until golden on each side, with the iconic white patches forming in the middle. Remove with a slotted spatula to drain on kitchen paper and keep covered while you are making the rest.

To serve, top with a tablespoon of sour cream and one of the stewed plums. Alternatively, dust with icing (confectioner's) sugar. Serve immediately.

Chapter 7

Homemade Cakes

We have reached the highest peak of our Romanian baking story: the homemade cakes, *prăjituri de casă*. Many cakes are made with *pandișpan*, a name that comes from *pain d'Espagne*, which is a sponge cake. In most recipes, the eggs are separated and the whites beaten to stiff peaks, then incorporated back into the cake batter. This makes the layers incredibly light. Other soft cakes, which are simply called *chec*, are loaf cakes – light and perfect with a cup of coffee.

Under the same name of *prăjitură*, there is a different type of recipe, made with a rich, crumbly and buttery dough, which is more like a biscuit. It is often spread with jam and topped with meringue, or layered with buttercream.

A distinct feature of homemade cakes is that people bake them in rectangular trays and cut them into rectangular slices or bars. *Prăjitură* are not usually round, although I have changed a couple of them for practical reasons. Once again, fermented dairy such as crème fraîche, sour cream and yoghurt help with the flavours and textures, as they do in so many recipes throughout the book. They are one of the main features of baking in Romania.

All recipes in this chapter are versatile, enabling you to master a few different types of cakes from where you can start experimenting. I have selected the ones that are representative for a certain style of *prăjitură*, and I haven't by any means included everything that we bake at home.

There is one powerful story in this chapter, that of Baron von Brukenthal in Sibiu (on page 181). As I was allowed to see some of the recipes in his 18th-century manuscript, I wanted to include one here and give you a taste of the past. You will find it extremely modern in its simplicity and in how quickly it comes together. It is an elegant almond bread pudding served with homemade gooseberry jam – Baron's favourite.

Saxon Rhubarb Cake

Prajitura săsească cu rabarbăr

I could have easily called this cake the Queen of Puddings of rural Transylvania. This recipe comes from Mălâncrav, one of the oldest Saxon villages in Transylvania, which used to have the largest German community in the region. In the summer, it is heaving with tourists. Denisa Babeş makes the best rhubarb cake in the village for the guests. The meringue should be caramelised and crisp on top, while the layer underneath should remain white, airy and light.

Serves 12

60 ml (2 fl oz/¼ cup) sunflower oil, plus extra for greasing
4 medium eggs, separated
110 g (3¾ oz/½ cup) caster (superfine) sugar
juice of ½ small lemon
1 teaspoon vanilla extract
130 ml (4½ fl oz/generous ½ cup) full-fat milk
160 g (5½ oz/1¼ cups) plain (all-purpose) flour
8 g (2½ teaspoons) baking powder
1 tablespoon fine semolina

For the filling

100 g (3½ oz) fresh rhubarb, cut into 1 cm (½ in) pieces

For the topping

(egg whites from the eggs above)
juice of ½ small lemon
125 g (4 oz/generous ½ cup) caster (superfine) sugar
1 teaspoon cornflour (cornstarch)

Preheat the oven to 200°C (non-fan)/400°F/gas 6. Grease and line a 20 x 30 x 4 cm (8 x 12 x 1½ in) aluminium baking tray (pan).

In a large bowl, whisk the egg yolks and sugar with the lemon juice and vanilla until they triple in volume. Add the milk and oil a couple of tablespoons at a time, alternating between them and whisking constantly. Incorporate well after each addition. Sift and fold in the flour gently together with the baking powder, then pour into the prepared baking tray. Sprinkle the semolina evenly on top, then dot the rhubarb on top in an even layer.

Bake on a lower shelf of the oven for 10 minutes until golden and slightly firm.

Meanwhile, make the meringue topping by whisking the egg whites in a large bowl to soft peaks. Add the lemon juice. Combine the sugar with the cornflour, and gradually add to the whites until they turn glossy.

Reduce the oven temperature to 160°C (non-fan)/320°F/gas 2, leaving the door open for a few seconds to allow the oven to cool.

Take the tray out and spoon the meringue topping evenly over the top of the cake. Bake for 20-25 minutes until the meringue looks golden.

Turn the heat off and leave the tray in the oven for the meringue to dry and get crisp. Allow to cool completely, then cut into slices and serve. Although not traditional, I usually serve it with poached rhubarb on the side.

Hazelnut and Prune Bars

Figaro

Although this cake is known as *Figaro*, there is no direct link to the mischievous character in Mozart's opera, other than it was probably easier to pronounce than the German *stangen* or *schnitten*, on which the recipe is based. It is typical of many cakes of German origin in Romania, with its sequence of layers, from the buttery biscuit, spread with a tangy jam, to the textured hazelnut meringue on top. If you learn to make this, you have the blueprint for many other cakes. In Romania, we love the version with plum butter, *magiun*, instead of jam.

Makes 14

For the dough
120 g (4 oz) unsalted
    butter, softened, plus extra
    for greasing
50 g (2 oz/¼ cup) caster
    (superfine) sugar
3 medium eggs, separated
200 g (7 oz/1⅔ cup) plain
    (all-purpose) flour
50 g (2 oz/½ cup)
    almond flour

For the filling
300 g (10½ oz) prunes
zest and juice of 2 medium
    lemons, or as needed
1 tablespoon rum or kirsch
    (optional) or water

For the topping
100 g (3½ oz/¾ cup)
    blanched hazelnuts
1 pinch of salt
(egg whites from the
    eggs above)
125 g (4 oz/generous ½ cup)
    caster (superfine) sugar

Start with the dough. In a mixing bowl, cream the butter with the sugar, then add the egg yolks one by one, incorporating well after each addition. Add both flours and mix until it forms a soft dough. Knead a couple of times, then wrap and place in the refrigerator for 30–40 minutes until firm.

Preheat the oven to 200°C (non-fan)/400°F/gas 6. Grease and line a 20 x 30 x 4 cm (8 x 12 x 1½ in) baking tray (pan).

While the oven is warming, spread the hazelnuts for the topping on a baking sheet and roast them in the warming oven to a rich golden colour. Sprinkle with a pinch of salt and set aside.

Roll out the dough to roughly the size of the baking tray, and evenly press it into the base of the tray. If it's too soft, place in the refrigerator or freezer until firm. Prick with a fork and bake for 20 minutes until golden.

Meanwhile, make the filling by blending all the ingredients to a spreadable consistency, adding more lemon juice if necessary.

Make the topping by whisking the egg whites in a large bowl to soft peaks. Add the sugar gradually and whisk until glossy. Chop the toasted hazelnuts and stir them in right at the end.

Reduce the oven temperature to 150°C (non-fan)/300°F/gas 1, leaving the door open for a few seconds to allow the oven to cool.

Take the tray out of the oven and spread the prune filling on top in a very thin layer. Spoon the hazelnut meringue evenly on top. Bake for a further 20 minutes.

Turn the heat off and allow to cool in the oven for 10 minutes.

Remove from the oven, transfer to a wooden board and slice the cake into bars while still warm. Leave to cool completely and serve.

Homemade Cakes

Apple and Caraway Loaf Cake

Chec cu mere si chimen

All over Romania, a *chec* has so many variations that I could easily write a whole chapter on it. Many people have their own favourite recipe, they bake it plain or marbled with cocoa powder, or dot it with fruit and serve it glazed or dusted with icing (confectioner's) sugar. The recipe here is my own contribution to this already varied collection, through which I wish to celebrate two important Romanian ingredients: apples and caraway seeds. The latter is a spice from Transylvania mostly used in savoury dishes, but works equally well in sweet recipes too. This is a cake that reminds me of home whenever I bake it.

Serves 10

115 g (3¾ oz) unsalted butter, softened, plus extra for greasing
150 g (5 oz/⅔ cup) golden caster (superfine) sugar
2 medium eggs
150 g (5 oz/1¼ cups) plain (all-purpose) flour
1 teaspoon baking powder
150 g (5 oz) Bramley apples, grated
1 tablespoon caraway seeds, lightly toasted

Preheat the oven to 180°C (non-fan)/350°F/gas 4. Grease and line a 10 x 21 cm (4 x 8¼ in) loaf tin (pan).

In a large bowl, cream the butter with the sugar until pale in colour and fluffy. Add the eggs one by one, incorporating well after each addition. Sift the flour with the baking powder on top and combine well. Fold in the grated apples together with the caraway seeds.

Pour the batter into the loaf tin and bake for 55 minutes on the lower shelf of the oven, covering the top with kitchen foil for the last 10 minutes.

Remove from the oven and transfer to a cooling rack after 5 minutes. Allow to cool completely before serving.

Cherry and Basil Sour Cream Cake

Prăjitură cu smântână, cireşe şi busuioc

I consider this to be a seasonal cake, mainly because people start baking it when the cherry and sour cherry season opens in early June, and stop when the damson and plum season ends in late October. The most popular one is made with sour cherries, although you will find it prepared not only with apricots and peaches, but also with rhubarb and soft fruit. This is an exceptional cake, the best of its kind in Romania.

Serves 6–8

3 tablespoons sunflower oil, plus extra for greasing
3 large eggs, separated
150 g (5 oz/⅔ cup) golden caster (superfine) sugar
100 g (3½ oz/scant ½ cup) sour cream
zest and juice of 1 medium lemon
1 tablespoon almond extract
150 g (5 oz/1¼ cups) plain (all-purpose) flour
½ teaspoon baking powder

To decorate

180 g (6½ oz) cherries, pitted
1 tablespoon chopped basil
1 tablespoon golden caster (superfine) sugar

To finish

icing (confectioner's) sugar, for dusting
1 teaspoon chopped basil

Note

The use of basil is a personal recommendation, since this herb plays a role in many traditions in the countryside, and it should do the same in cookery. However, you can leave it out completely, or just sprinkle a little on top before serving.

Preheat the oven to 180°C (non-fan)/350°F/gas 4. Grease and line a 18 x 24 x 6 cm (7 x 9½ x 2½ in) baking tin (pan).

In a large bowl, whisk the egg whites to soft peaks, then add the sugar little by little until the peaks are firm and hold their shape. Beat in the egg yolks, one at a time.

In a separate bowl, stir together the oil, sour cream, lemon zest and juice and almond extract, then whisk it into the cake batter. Sift in the flour and baking powder, folding gently.

Just before you are ready to bake the cake, toss the cherries and basil with the tablespoon of sugar. Pour the batter into the baking tin and add the cherries on top, pressing them slightly into the batter. Bake for 35 minutes.

Remove from the oven and allow to cool in the tin for 10 minutes. Peel off the baking paper and transfer to a cooling rack. Dust with icing sugar and sprinkle with the chopped basil, then cut into 6–8 large slices.

Baron von Brukenthal

× × × × × × × × × × × × × × × × × × × ×

Baron Samuel of Brukenthal was the Governor of Transylvania for 10 years, from 1777–87, having his official residence in the capital Sibiu. He was born in Nocrich, a Saxon village near Sibiu, and was educated at the best European universities of the time, absorbing the ideals of the Age of Enlightenment, which were sweeping through the continent. Empress Maria Theresa of Austria asked him to be her personal advisor, and he was later appointed Governor of the Great Principality of Transylvania. Only now was he able to bring back home his visionary ideals of a new society governed by education and science.

As a private person, he led his life according to Saxon principles based on simplicity and frugality. He never drank alcohol, preferring fresh water brought to his house every day from a mountain spring outside the town. At his mansion in the countryside in Avrig, not only did he embrace the art of landscaping, inspiring the entire noble class to take up this new trend, but he also turned the gardens into a Siebenbürgische Eden, a Transylvanian Paradise. He experimented with different agricultural techniques, planting potatoes, sugar cane, beetroot and asparagus, and taught the local farmers how to grow them. This is how the potato was introduced to Transylvania, through what must have been the first agricultural lessons of the times. Wanting to improve the quality of milk, he brought Egyptian white buffalo to Saxon villages, which explains the presence of their rich dairy produce in Transylvanian cookery.

Being fond of jams and confitures, the Baron decided to build a separate kitchen especially for 'boiling sugar', as he called it. It was here that all sweet preserves were prepared using only fruit grown at the estate in the countryside. His favourites were cherry confiture, fig jam with figs from the orangeries, gooseberry and rosehip jams and redcurrant cordial. The Baron was so particular about them that he even liked to take stock of all the jars in the pantry himself.

As a political figure, he had to rise to the demands of his job and built the most imposing palace in Transylvania in a late Baroque style. Here, he collected art, books and engravings, musical instruments, rare ancient coins and watches. In his will he made it clear that the palace and the collections had to be turned into a museum, the first of its kind in Transylvania and in south-east Europe.

Only one manuscript was found from the Baron's kitchens, which contained hand-written recipes. Sadly, nothing survived from the banquet menus. I was lucky to be sent a few of these recipes and was surprised by the variety of soufflé-style puddings, made with bread and almonds, sometimes with a caramel topping. I suspect that some fruit sauce or jam would have been a regular accompaniment too.

Brukenthal Bread Puddings with Gooseberry Jam

Budincă Brukenthal de pâine și migdale cu gem de agrișe

✕ ✕ ✕ ✕ ✕ ✕ ✕ ✕ ✕ ✕ ✕ ✕ ✕ ✕ ✕ ✕ ✕ ✕ ✕

Here is a recipe inspired by the Baron's recipes, easy to make and served with his favourite gooseberry jam. The almonds would have been from his trees at the country home.

Makes 4

- 2½ tablespoons unsalted butter, softened, plus extra for greasing
- 50 g (2 oz/½ cup) ground almonds, plus extra for dusting the ramekins
- 80 g (3 oz) white bread, about 4 slices without crusts, cut into 1 cm (½ in) cubes
- 300 ml (10 fl oz/1¼ cups) full-fat milk
- 2 eggs, separated
- 2 generous tablespoons honey
- 1 teaspoon almond extract
- ½ teaspoon ground ginger
- ¼ teaspoon ground nutmeg
- ¼ teaspoon ground cardamom
- 1 pinch of freshly ground black pepper

To serve

- 400 g (14 oz) red gooseberries
- 100 g (3½ oz/scant ½ cup) golden caster (superfine) sugar
- zest and juice of 1 lemon

Preheat the oven to 180°C (non-fan)/350°F/gas 4. Grease the inside of 4 ramekins, 8 cm (3 in) in diameter and 5 cm (2 in) deep, and coat with ground almonds.

Put the bread pieces in a food processor. Bring the milk to the boil in a small pan, then pour it over the bread. Leave to cool for 15 minutes, then blitz for a few seconds to make a smooth paste. Add the butter, mixing well, followed by the egg yolks and honey. Add the almond extract, ground almonds and spices, and combine well.

In a bowl, whisk the egg whites to stiff peaks, then fold into the batter.

Bring a kettle to the boil.

Fill each ramekin all the way up with the batter, then place them in a large roasting tin and put it in the oven. Pour boiling water from the kettle into the roasting tin to cover the base (don't get any in the ramekins!). Bake on a lower shelf in the oven for 30–40 minutes until golden on top.

Prepare the gooseberry jam by stewing the gooseberries in a pan with the sugar and lemon zest and juice over a medium heat for 15 minutes. Set aside.

When the puddings are ready, serve them immediately with a teaspoon of gooseberry jam in the middle of each.

Homemade Cakes

Honey Roulade with Quince Jam

Ruladă cu miere și gem de gutui

Apiaries in this part of Eastern Europe have been highly appreciated since ancient times, and through the centuries honey was often included on the list of tithes and regular tributes sent as payment for taxes or tokens of submission to the ruling empires. Today, wild flower meadows, linden and acacia trees are a haven for bees, and the honey produced in Romania is one of the best in the world. I chose to complement the honey in this recipe with another ancient ingredient: quince, which appears in old cookery books as often as apples do today. This roulade is very delicate in flavour.

Serves 10

1½ tablespoons unsalted
   butter, plus extra
   for greasing
1½ tablespoons honey
3 medium eggs, separated
100 g (3½ oz/scant ½ cup)
   caster (superfine) sugar,
   plus extra for dusting
1 teaspoon vanilla extract
1 teaspoon vanilla bean paste
100 g (3½ oz/generous
   ¾ cup) plain (all-purpose)
   flour, sifted
icing (confectioner's) sugar,
   for dusting

For the quince jam

100 ml (3½ fl oz/scant ½ cup)
   water
100 g (3½ oz/scant ½ cup)
   caster (superfine) sugar
300 g (10½ oz) quince,
   grated with skin on
zest and juice of 1 lemon

Preheat the oven to 180°C (non-fan)/350°F/gas 4. Grease and line a 20 x 30 x 2 cm (8 x 12 x ¾ in) baking tray (pan).

In a small pan, heat the honey and butter, then allow to cool for 10 minutes.

In a large bowl, beat the egg yolks with half the quantity of sugar, then add the honey mixture and both types of vanilla and combine well. Mix in the sifted flour.

In a separate bowl, whisk the egg whites to soft peaks, then add the rest of the sugar and whisk to stiff peaks. Mix a quarter of the whites into the egg yolk batter to loosen the mixture, then gently fold in the rest of the whites, trying not to deflate them too much.

Spread the mixture over the prepared tray and bake for 12 minutes.

Meanwhile, cut a sheet of baking paper a little larger than the tray and sprinkle it with caster sugar.

Remove the tray from the oven and gently turn the sponge onto the sugar-sprinkled baking paper. Make a shallow incision along one of the shorter sides, 1 cm (½ in) in from the edge, and roll up the sponge together with the baking paper from that edge and all the way up. Allow to cool completely.

Make the quince jam by bringing the water and sugar to the boil in a medium pan. Turn the heat down to medium and add the grated quince. Cook for 15 minutes, stirring often. Towards the end of the cooking time, add the lemon zest and juice. The jam should be thick, with a spreadable consistency. Turn off the heat, place a damp dish towel on top, and allow to cool. If after cooling it is too thick to spread, warm it gently in the pan.

When the sponge has cooled, unroll it, peel away the baking paper and spread with the jam. Roll it up again and dust with icing sugar. You can serve it right away or – better – wait for another hour to allow the jam to set properly.

Walnut Cake with Sour Chantilly Cream and Drunken Cherries

Prăjitură de nucă

This is an unusually thin, rectangular cake that is perfect for when you like to end a meal on a light note. It is gluten-free by accident, only because walnuts often replace flour, partially or entirely, in many Romanian cakes or biscuits. The recipe belongs to Rebeka Stamate, who has collected many recipes throughout the years from both the Hungarian and Romanian sides of her family. According to her, the cake can be topped with cream and either jam or fruit from a compote. I use ruby red drunken cherries, which are my favourite. The cake is refreshing and not overly sweet.

Serves 8

butter or oil, for greasing
4 medium eggs, separated
80 g (3 oz/⅓ cup) golden caster (superfine) sugar
1 teaspoon almond extract
100 g (3½ oz/1 cup) walnuts, finely chopped or ground in a food processor

For the topping

50 ml (1¾ fl oz/3½ tablespoons) double (heavy) cream
30 g (1 oz/3 tablespoons) golden caster (superfine) sugar
120 ml (4 fl oz/½ cup) sour cream
1 teaspoon vanilla bean paste
1 teaspoon almond extract

For the drunken cherries

300 g (10½ oz) frozen cherries, defrosted and drained
75 ml (2½ fl oz/5 tablespoons) Amaretto liqueur
1 tablespoon kirsch (alternatively use 300 g/ 10½ oz store-bought cherries in kirsch or leftovers from making Romanian *vișinată*)

If you are making your own drunken cherries, use a deep bowl and combine all the ingredients. Leave to infuse until you are ready to serve.

Preheat the oven to 180°C (non-fan)/350°F/gas 4. Grease and line a 20 x 30 cm (8 x 12 in) cake tin (pan).

In a large bowl, beat the egg yolks with 50g (2 oz/¼ cup) of the sugar and the almond extract until pale. Incorporate the walnuts.

In a separate bowl, whisk the egg whites to soft peaks, then add the remaining 30 g (1 oz/3 tablespoons) of the sugar, whisking to stiff peaks. Fold the whites into the walnut mixture, then pour into the prepared tin.

Bake for 25 minutes on a low shelf until a skewer inserted in the cake comes out clean. Remove from the oven and tin and allow to cool completely on a wire rack.

Just before you are ready to serve, make the topping by whisking all the ingredients together. Drain the cherries, reserving the liquid. Evenly spread the sour cream over the cake and cut into rectangular slices. Serve with some cherries on the side (or on top) and drizzle over a little of the juice.

Crumble Cake with Grape Jam

Prăjitură fragedă cu magiun de struguri

✛✛✛✛✛✛✛✛✛✛✛✛✛✛✛✛✛✛✛✛✛

You will find the word *magiun* in many Romanian baking recipes, usually referring to a set, thick and tangy plum butter. Traditionally, it was made without sugar, the sweetness coming only from slow cooking and concentrating the natural sugar from the fruit. In the past, *magiun* was made from a variety of different fruit, sometimes even a medley depending on what people had in their gardens. Historian Andrei Oișteanu finds it mentioned in 1716 as *madjoon*, when a Greek nobleman in the Principality of Moldavia sent it as a special gift to the Patriarch of Jerusalem, with a private note. It read '… made as if it were for myself, the way I know you enjoy it'. His version contained opium, a concoction made with added sugar and spices, which was considered to be a medicine. Across the Carpathian mountains in Transylvania, similar sugary remedies were made from plants or fruit, known as *lictar* or *povidlă*, luckily with no other additions.

Serves 8

200 g (7 oz) unsalted butter, cold and diced into 1 cm (½ in) cubes, plus extra for greasing
350 g (12 oz/scant 3 cups) plain (all-purpose) flour, plus extra for dusting
50 g (2 oz/¼ cup) golden caster (superfine) sugar
1 medium egg, plus 1 yolk
50 ml (1¾ fl oz/ 3½ tablespoons) sour cream
1 tablespoon water

For the filling

700 g (1 lb 9 oz) green and red grapes
1 tablespoon honey
1 tablespoon water
zest and juice of 2 limes

Alternative fillings

Use apples and walnuts, as per recipe on page 57
Use *magiun de prune*, plum butter, as per recipe on page 110

In a large bowl, rub the butter into the flour until they resemble coarse breadcrumbs or use a food processor. Add the sugar, eggs, sour cream and water and mix until they form a dough. Turn onto the work surface and press with your fingertips, bringing the dough together with your palms and trying not to knead. Wrap in clingfilm (plastic wrap) and place in the refrigerator for 15 minutes.

Preheat the oven to 200°C (non-fan)/400°F/gas 6. Grease and line a 18 x 24 x 6 cm (7 x 9½ x 2½ in) baking tray (pan).

In a small pan, bring the filling ingredients to the boil, then simmer until the grapes are soft, crushing them lightly with a fork or a potato masher. Set aside to cool.

Divide the dough in half and place one half in the freezer. Roll out the other half on a lightly floured work surface to roughly the size of the baking tray. Gently press it it into the tray to reach all corners and prick with a fork. Bake on the lower shelf of the oven for 15 minutes, or until it starts to turn golden.

Remove from the oven and spread the filling on top, then grate over the remaining dough from the freezer. Return the tray to the oven and bake for a further 25 minutes, or until the top is golden.

Lemon Cake

Prăjitură cu lamâie

This layered cake goes by the name of *Lamâița,* and is typical of a homemade *prăjitură cu cremă* in Romania, with custard buttercream. In this particular case, the custard is made only with milk and flour and no eggs, the finesse coming from the creaminess of the butter. Make sure it is properly set before slicing. Even then, store the slices in the refrigerator, otherwise the filling turns soft very quickly.

Serves 8

100 g (3½ oz) unsalted butter, softened, plus extra for greasing
35 g (1¼ oz/3 tablespoons) golden caster (superfine) sugar
1 medium egg
250 g (9 oz/2 cups) plain (all-purpose) flour, plus extra for dusting
100 ml (3½ fl oz/scant ½ cup) full-fat milk
½ teaspoon baking powder
icing (confectioner's) sugar, for dusting

For the buttercream

150 ml (5 fl oz/scant ⅔ cup) full-fat milk
25 g (¾ oz/3 tablespoons) plain (all-purpose) flour
75 g (2½ oz/⅓ cup) golden caster (superfine) sugar
zest and juice of 1 large lemon
90 g (3¼ oz) unsalted butter, diced

In a large bowl, cream the butter with the sugar until pale, then mix in the egg. Add the flour, milk and baking powder, and combine well with a spoon. It will resemble a thick paste. Cover the bowl and place in the refrigerator for 1 hour, after which knead the dough briefly and place in the freezer for 10 minutes.

Meanwhile, make the buttercream. In a bowl, gradually mix the milk with the flour to avoid forming lumps. Transfer the mixture to a pan and simmer until it has the consistency of extra-thick double (heavy) cream. Remove from the heat and add the sugar. Cool to a lukewarm temperature, then mix in the lemon zest and juice, and the butter. Allow to cool completely in the refrigerator.

Preheat the oven to 180°C (non-fan)/350°F/gas 4. Grease and line the base of a 18 x 24 cm (7 x 9½ in) baking tray (pan).

Flour your work surface generously, divide the dough into three equal parts and roll out one piece to the size of the baking tray. Place the other pieces of dough in the refrigerator while you work. Arrange the dough neatly in the tray, prick it with a fork and bake for 10 minutes. It needs to look quite pale, somewhere between white and a very light golden colour.

Transfer to a cooling rack, then repeat the process with the other two pieces of dough.

When the baking tray has cooled, line it with a large piece of clingfilm (plastic wrap), so that the sides overhang the edges.

Take the buttercream out of the refrigerator and very briefly whisk to a stiff consistency. Place one pastry sheet on the base of the lined tray, spread it with half of the buttercream, then repeat with a second layer, using up the rest of the buttercream. Top with a final pastry layer, cover with clingfilm and allow to set for at least 2 hours or ideally overnight.

When ready to serve, remove from the tray, trim the edges, cut into bars and dust with icing sugar. Store in the refrigerator.

Homemade Cakes

Chapter 8

Layer Cakes and Nostalgic Patisserie Treats

It often happened that the most iconic cakes created in the patisserie shops of Vienna, Budapest and Bucharest became so popular that home bakers started to include them in their repertoire for special occasions. This is the case with *Gerbeaud* cake, or Greta Garbo as it is known in Romania, and others such as *Rigo*, *Dobos*, *Sacher* and *Eszterházy* cakes. In the late 19th century, there was a proliferation of cakes named after their creators, current events, actresses, noble families, politicians, royals, ballerinas, opera singers and, in many other cases, after family members. I have given you the recipe for the first two (*Gerbeaud* on page 204 and *Rigo* on page 206), as they just happen to be very easy to make, and each is representative of its own type of fancy cakes.

In Romania, round, layered cakes are called *torturi*, as in tortes. The word comes from *turta*, which still exists in our cookery repertoire as a round flatbread. With some exceptions, there are two main types of *torturi*: one that uses génoise sponge or meringue dacquoise layers, which are often drizzled with rum syrup and sandwiched with buttercream; the other is based on mousse creams layered with ladyfinger biscuits. These cakes represent the panache of the urban middle classes, and none are to be found in rural, traditional cookery.

During the Communist regime that ended in 1989, patisserie shops had known ups and downs, often having to cope with a lack of ingredients, which affected the quality of their products. Nostalgia works in curious ways, and there are still a few cakes that have stood the test of time. Every Romanian will remember *savarine*, *éclairs* and *choux à la crème*. I have included the recipes in this chapter, since paradoxically (or perhaps not) they taste better when made at home than when bought in a shop.

Coffee Cream Puffs

Choux-à-la-crème cu cafea

When I was a teenager, I used to save my pocket money to buy cream puffs, and almost every time I'd get a couple of coffee éclairs too. Here I make both in one recipe, which reminds me of my beloved Bucharest and the patisserie shop near my high school.

Makes 12

For the choux pastry
170 ml (6 fl oz/¾ cup) water
45 g (1¾ oz) unsalted butter
80 g (3 oz/⅔ cup) plain
    (all-purpose) flour
2 medium eggs

For the filling
300 ml (10 fl oz/1¼ cups)
    double (heavy) cream
40 g (1½ oz/⅓ cup) icing
    (confectioner's) sugar, plus
    extra for dusting
1 teaspoon vanilla bean paste
5 teaspoons powdered
    instant coffee

Preheat the oven to 200°C (non-fan)/400°F/gas 6. Line a baking sheet with baking paper.

First, make the pastry. Bring the water and butter to the boil in a medium pan. Sift in the flour and whisk vigorously until the mixture comes away from the sides of the pan and looks shiny. Remove from the heat and use a wooden spoon to quickly stir in the eggs, one by one. The batter should be thick, barely falling off the spoon, but easy to pipe.

Spoon the batter into a piping bag fitted with a 1 cm (½ in) star nozzle. Pipe the pastry onto the prepared baking sheet in 3–4 cm (1½ in) circles, leaving only little gaps in the middles, then pipe on top again to make a double-decker circle. Repeat until you use up all the mixture. Leave a gap between each choux, because they will expand.

Bake for 25 minutes, or until golden, then open the oven door slightly and bake for a further 5 minutes. Turn the oven off and take out the choux. Using a wooden skewer, poke several holes around the sides. Return them to the turned-off oven and allow them to crisp up for a further 10 minutes. Remove from the oven and cool on a wire rack.

Make the filling by whisking the cream to soft peaks in a large bowl. Add the icing sugar, vanilla and instant coffee, and whisk until the peaks hold their shape. Transfer the mixture to a piping bag fitted with a 1 cm (½ in) star nozzle (alternatively, you can just use a teaspoon for the next stage).

Cut each bun in half horizontally and pipe some filling on the bottom half of each bun. Place the other halves on top and dust with icing sugar. They are ready to serve.

Diplomat Cake with Rum-Roasted Pineapple

Tort Diplomat cu ananas și rom

This cake has often been associated with New Year's Eve in Romania. During the Communist regime, the importance of Christmas was downplayed in favour of a non-religious day, seen as more suitable for a society geared towards modernity and 'scientific progress'. In reality, it was the only time of the year when we saw lemons, oranges and pineapples, the latter usually in a can – the proof that exotic, luxury goods were available to everyone in socialist Romania. Today, we make this cake on many other occasions and some people like to decorate it in intricate patterns made with different slices of fruit. When kept simple using natural ingredients, the cake is a feather-light, exotic pineapple mousse resting on airy sponge fingers, all infused by the aromatic rum.

Serves 8

1 x 432 g (14 oz) can pineapple pieces in syrup
6 tablespoons dark rum
1 x 432 g (14 oz) can pineapple slices in syrup
4 gelatine leaves
4 medium egg yolks
50 g (2 oz/¼ cup) caster (superfine) sugar
1 teaspoon vanilla extract
125 g (4 oz/generous ½ cup) crème fraîche
250 ml (8½ fl oz/1 cup) double (heavy) cream

To assemble

100 g (3½ oz) sponge fingers (recipe on page 32 or use store-bought)
6 tablespoons dark rum, or to taste
150 ml (5 fl oz/scant ⅔ cup) double (heavy) cream
2 generous tablespoons icing (confectioner's) sugar
dried or glacé cherries, to decorate

Preheat the oven to 220°C (non-fan)/430°F/gas 8. Line a baking sheet with non-stick paper.

Drain the pineapple pieces and reserve the syrup. Dice into even smaller pieces, place on the baking sheet and drizzle with 2 tablespoons of the rum. Roast for 20 minutes, or until they start to caramelise around the edges. Remove from the oven and set aside.

Re-line the baking sheet. Drain the pineapple slices and reserve the syrup. Roast the slices whole, brushed with 2 tablespoons of the rum, for 20 minutes. Remove from the oven and set aside. Cut in half when cool enough to handle.

Meanwhile, soak the gelatine leaves in cold water.

In a large bowl, whisk the egg yolks with the sugar. Measure 180 ml (6 fl oz/¾ cup) of the reserved pineapple syrup into a pan and warm through. Pour the warm syrup over the eggs, whisking all the time. Return the mixture to the pan over a medium heat and cook until it thickens, stirring continuously. Remove from the heat, stir in the vanilla and set aside for 5 minutes.

Squeeze the water out of the gelatine leaves and add them to the custard, mixing well. Leave to cool completely.

In a bowl, combine the crème fraîche with the roasted, chopped pineapple pieces and remaining 2 tablespoons of rum, then mix in the custard.

In a separate bowl, whisk the double cream to firm peaks, then fold it into the custard mixture. Set aside.

To assemble, use a 20 cm (8 in) loose-bottomed diameter cake tin (pan) or line it with clingfilm (plastic wrap). Arrange the sponge fingers on the bottom of the tin to form a base – you will

need to break a few to fit them in the gaps. Brush generously with
4 tablespoons of the rum. Pour the pineapple custard cream on top
and refrigerate for at least 2 hours or overnight.

Remove the cake from the tin and place on a serving plate. Whisk
the cream with the icing sugar to firm peaks, add the remaining
2 tablespoons of rum, then spread over the top and sides of the cake.
Arrange the half slices of pineapple around the base, placing a cherry
in the hole of each. Decorate the top of the cake with more cherries.

Layer Cakes and Nostalgic Patisserie Treats

Mini Savarin Cakes with Elderflower Syrup and Summer Berries

Savarine cu sirop de soc și fructe de pădure

Savarins have been very popular desserts in Romania since the beginning of the 20th century, when the sophistication of the Belle Epoque was reverberating from Paris to the streets of Bucharest. Its origin goes back to the Duke Stanislas Leszczynski, former King of Poland and Lithuania, who spent his exile in France and used to complain about his beloved home-country *Kugelhopf* being too dry. His French pastry chef Nicolas Stohrer, who later opened the first ever patisserie shop in Paris, decided to fix it and soaked it in Malaga wine, which the Duke – already partial to good alcohol – adored. This recipe inspired two famous desserts: *baba-au-rhum* and savarin. The latter used no raisins and was soaked in kirsch, and was named after the renowned French gastronome Brillat-Savarin. My recipe follows in these footsteps with only tiny changes in flavour, also offering you a non-alcoholic option.

Recipe overleaf

Continued

Makes 12

For the dough

75 g (2½ oz) unsalted
  butter, softened, plus
  extra for greasing
200 g (7 oz/1⅓ cups) plain
  (all-purpose) flour
80 g (3 oz/⅔ cup) strong
  bread flour
30 g (1 oz/3 tablespoons)
  golden caster
  (superfine) sugar
12 g (1⅔ sachets) fast-action
  dried yeast
120 ml (4 fl oz/½ cup) full-fat
  milk, lukewarm
2 medium eggs, lightly beaten
1 teaspoon almond extract
vegetable oil, for greasing

For the syrup

300 ml (10 fl oz/1¼ cups)
  elderflower cordial/syrup
200 ml (7 fl oz/ scant 1 cup)
  water
zest and juice of 1 large lemon
1 teaspoon almond extract
75 ml (2½ fl oz/5 tablespoons)
  brandy or kirsch (optional,
  can be replaced with water)

To serve

100 ml (3½ fl oz/scant ½ cup)
  double (heavy) cream
1 teaspoon vanilla bean
  extract
100 g (3½ oz) soft summer
  fruit, fresh or defrosted
extra lemon zest

You will need twelve 9 cm (4 in) fluted brioche moulds, generously greased with butter.

First, make the dough. In a stand mixer, combine the flours with the sugar, yeast and milk. Mix in the eggs, then add the butter little by little, followed by the almond extract. Beat for 8 minutes on medium speed until it looks and feels like a very thick cream. Divide the mixture between the prepared moulds, filling them two-thirds of the way up. Place the moulds on a baking sheet, cover with an oiled piece of clingfilm (plastic wrap) and then with a light dish towel. Leave to rise in a warm place for 1 hour, or until the dough reaches the rim of the moulds.

Meanwhile, preheat the oven to 180°C (non-fan)/350°F/gas 4.

Remove the clingfilm and bake the savarins on the lower shelf of the oven for 20 minutes, or until golden. Remove from the moulds carefully once they are safe to touch. Allow to cool completely (some people leave them overnight).

Make the syrup by gently warming all the ingredients together without boiling. If you are using brandy or kirsch, add it after you take the pan off the heat. Taste and add more if you like. Allow to cool slightly, then add the savarins and leave them to soak in the syrup for 15 minutes, turning them from time to time. Work in batches, if needed.

When you are ready to serve, whip the cream and add the vanilla. Place each savarin on a plate and top with a small amount of the cream. Add a few summer berries and a little lemon zest and drizzle more syrup around the base, if you have any left.

Budapest Gerbeaud Cake with Walnuts and Apricot Jam

Garbo prăjitură cu nucă și gem de caise

In Romania, we call this cake *Garbo*, but it also goes by the name of *zserbó* in Hungarian homes and *scherbo* in German homes, all versions of the the the cake's original name: *Gerbeaud*. The cake was created by the Swiss Emile Gerbeaud at his internationally acclaimed café and pastry shop in Budapest, Hungary. At the end of the 19th century, he had 150 employees, producing some of the most exquisite desserts in the Austro-Hungarian empire. The cake turned out to be so easy to make, with the layers and filling being baked at the same time, that it was immediately adopted by home bakers. The café still exists today in all its glory and sophistication, serving their original recipe alongside equally loved *Dobos* and *Esterhazy Tortes*, to the jazz tunes of live gypsy music.

Serves 16

250 g (9 oz) unsalted butter, softened, plus extra for greasing
500 g (1 lb 2 oz/4 cups) plain (all-purpose) flour
50 g (2 oz/¼ cup) caster (superfine) sugar
10 g (1½ sachets) fast-action dried yeast
zest of 1 orange
1 medium egg, plus 1 yolk
2 tablespoons sour cream
1 tablespoon full-fat milk

For the filling

200 g (7 oz/generous ½ cup) apricot jam
150 g (5 oz/1¼ cups) chopped walnuts
25 g (¾ oz/2 tablespoons) caster (superfine) sugar

For the topping

100 g (3½ oz) dark chocolate
25 g (¾ oz) unsalted butter
70 ml (2½ fl oz/5 tablespoons) water

Grease and line the bottom of a 20 x 30 x 4 cm (8 x 12 x 1½ in) baking tray (pan).

In a large bowl, mix the butter and flour to coarse crumbs. Add the sugar, yeast, orange zest, egg and yolk, and mix again briefly, then add the sour cream and milk. Knead for another 2 minutes until the dough looks smooth. Divide into 3 equal parts.

Roll out the first piece of dough to the size of the baking tray, trimming if necessary and using the trimmings to fill in any gaps. Press gently with your fingertips to make an even layer. Spread half of the apricot jam on top. Mix the chopped walnuts with the sugar, then sprinkle half of the mixture on top of the jam layer.

Repeat the above steps with the second piece of dough and the remaining apricot jam and walnut mixture, then finish by rolling out the final piece of dough and placing it on top. Cover with a dish towel and leave to prove in a warm place for 45 minutes.

Meanwhile, preheat the oven to 190°C (non-fan)/375°F/gas 5.

Bake for 35 minutes, or until dark golden.

Take the cake out of the oven and while it is still warm turn carefully onto a cooling rack. Leave to cool completely, ideally overnight.

To make the topping, heat all the ingredients in a pan until smooth, then allow to cool to a spreadable consistency. Spread the chocolate glaze on top of the cake and allow to cool for 10 minutes. With a sharp knife, trim the edges of the cake, then slice into 16 small rectangles.

Chocolate Mousse Torte Rigo Jancsi

Tort de ciocolată Rigo Jancsi

This is a famous Hungarian chocolate mousse cake that has entered the baking repertoire of families in Transylvania through the Magyar communities who live there. Everyone I have spoken to includes it on their list of 'Sunday cakes', since the recipe is easy to follow and is also associated with an incredible event from the past. It is a love story that scandalised and excited the high society of the time. Rigo Jancsi was a gypsy violinist, who by 1895 had become a celebrity in Paris due to his brilliant playing. Hungarian Romany music was highly regarded in Europe, and it was fashionable in restaurants to invite a band to play live for the guests. When dining out one evening with her husband, Princess Chimay fell in love with the good-looking, passionate Rigo, and they eloped on Christmas Day 1896, sending ripples of shock through both Paris and Budapest. The event fired up everyone's imagination, including a Hungarian pastry chef who created this torte in their honour. Home bakers made it their own, and it is popular in many Hungarian homes and patisseries. It is an intense, deeply rich chocolate mousse cake, which I have modified slightly to make gluten-free.

Makes 8 slices or 16 batons

For the mousse filling

500 ml (17 fl oz/2 cups) double (heavy) cream
300 g (10½ oz) dark chocolate (75–85% cocoa solids), finely chopped
25 g (¾ oz/2½ tablespoons) golden caster (superfine) sugar
35 g (1¼ oz/¼ cup) cocoa powder
2 teaspoons rum (optional)

For the layers

4 medium eggs, separated
65 g (2¼ oz/generous ¼ cup) caster (superfine) sugar
1 tablespoon honey
20 g (¾ oz/scant ¼ cup) cornflour (cornstarch)
2 tablespoons cocoa powder, plus extra for dusting

Preheat the oven to 190°C (non-fan)/375°F/gas 5. Grease and line a 18 x 24 x 6 cm (7 x 9½ x 2½ in) baking tray.

Make the mousse filling by heating the double cream gently in a small pan. Place the chopped chocolate and sugar in a bowl and pour the hot cream on top. Stir to a smooth consistency, then mix in the cocoa powder and the rum, if using. Place in the refrigerator while you make the cake layers.

To make the layers, whisk the egg yolks with half of the sugar and the honey until pale. In a separate bowl, whisk the egg whites with the remaining sugar to stiff peaks. Fold in the egg yolk mixture, then sift in the cornflour together with the cocoa. Fold carefully until the ingredients are well combined.

Spoon half of the mixture in the prepared baking tray, gently blending in any of the meringue bubbles that may still be visible. Even the top with a palette knife or the back of a spoon and bake for 10 minutes.

Remove from the oven and lift the cake with the baking paper onto a cooking rack.

Line the tray again and repeat with the remaining batter. Turn both cakes and gently peel off the baking paper. Ensure they have completely cooled before you start assembling the cake.

When the mousse filling is cold, whisk to soft peaks and it is ready to use. Line the same baking tray with clingfilm (plastic wrap). Place one cake layer in the tray and evenly spread over the mousse filling.

Place the second cake layer on top, pressing gently. Allow to set in the refrigerator for at least 2 hours.

When ready to serve, remove the cake from the baking tray, dust with cocoa powder, trim the edges and slice into 8 generous portions or 16 batons. Bring to room temperature before serving. You can serve alongside a teaspoon of cherry jam and unsweetened whipped cream, if you like. Some people prefer to cover the top with chocolate glaze, in which case you can use the recipe on page 204.

Layer Cakes and Nostalgic Patisserie Treats

Upside-Down Pear and Sage Cake

Tort de pere busuioace cu foi de salvie

Romanian pears were the most perfumed, sweet and delicate fruit of my childhood. I'm using them in this caramel cake alongside an important herb in our cuisine: sage. Although not used in sweet dishes, I wanted to add the subtle, aromatic bitterness of sage to balance the sweetness of the caramel. This is an elegant, thin cake, which is often served with whipped cream.

Serves 8

For the pears
3–4 Williams/Bartlett pears
    (not too ripe)
1 tablespoon verjuice or juice
    of 1 lemon

For the caramel
150 g (5 oz/⅔ cup) golden
    caster (superfine) sugar
60 g (2¼ oz) unsalted butter
5–6 sage leaves
1 teaspoon ground ginger

For the cake
2 medium eggs
75 g (2½ oz/⅓ cup) golden
    caster (superfine) sugar
20 g (¾ oz) unsalted butter,
    melted, plus extra
    for greasing
65 g (2¼ oz/½ cup) plain
    (all-purpose) flour

To serve
25 g (¾ oz/¼ cup)
    chopped hazelnuts
whipped cream (optional)

Preheat the oven to 200°C (non-fan)/400°F/gas 6.

Peel the pears, then cut them in half, remove the core and the stems. Set aside.

Next, make the caramel. In a pan, melt the sugar until golden, then add the butter and cook until it is a deep golden colour. Pour the caramel into a 20 cm (8 in) diameter metal pie dish, no deeper than 14 cm (5½ in). Add the sage leaves and ginger, then place the pears in the caramel, cut-sides down. Bake for 10 minutes.

Meanwhile, make the cake batter. In a large bowl, whisk the eggs with the sugar until pale, about 5 minutes. The mixture should be velvet-like; if you lift some of it with the whisk, it should fall back in thick ribbons, sitting on top of the mixture for a few moments. Carefully fold in the melted butter, then the flour.

Take the pears out of the oven and reduce the heat to 170°C (non-fan)/340°F/gas 3.

Brush the pears with the verjuice (or lemon juice), then pour half of the cake batter over the pears. Use a large spoon to carefully push the batter in between the pears and around the sides, otherwise the mixture will sit on top. Pour over the rest of the batter, distribute it evenly and level the top with a spatula. Work very gently. Bake for 25 minutes.

Remove from the oven and very carefully run a buttered knife around the edges. Rest for 5 minutes, then put a plate on top of the pan and quickly turn it upside down to reveal the cake. Allow to cool completely.

Serve with a sprinkle of hazelnuts and a dollop of whipped cream, if you like.

PERE DULCI
10 lei/Kg

Double Chocolate Cake

Amandine

More is more in this famous Romanian cake, a layered treat of light cocoa sponge and silky buttercream. This cake appeared in patisserie shops around 1960, during the Communist regime, so many of us grew up eating it, even when the penury of ingredients in the following years saw it being drenched in sugar syrup, with the filling made of fondant and cocoa powder. But we loved that. This recipe is a little more honourable, and I have included an option for glazing that I know so many people long for. For an intense cocoa flavour and a less sweet glaze, the second option is a good alternative.

Serves 8

For the cake
unsalted butter, for greasing
4 medium eggs, separated
80 g (3 oz/⅓ cup) caster
 (superfine) sugar
100 g (3½ oz/generous ¾ cup)
 plain (all-purpose) flour
25 g (¾ oz/scant ¼ cup)
 cocoa powder

For the syrup
150 g (5 oz/⅔ cup) caster
 (superfine) sugar
120 ml (4 fl oz/½ cup) hot water
1 tablespoon Angostura bitters
 (or Amaro, Campari or
 Fernet Branca)

For the buttercream
200 g (7 oz) soft unsalted butter
75 g (2½ oz/scant ⅔ cup) icing
 (confectioner's) sugar
25 g (¾ oz/scant ¼ cup)
 cocoa powder
1–3 tablespoons full-fat milk
 (optional: replace some of the
 milk with Angostura bitters)

Glaze option 1
150 g (5 oz) royal icing, diced
7 tablespoons water
2 tablespoons cocoa powder

Glaze option 2
100 ml (3½ fl oz/scant ½ cup)
 full-fat milk, warm
100 g (3½ oz/generous ¾ cup)
 icing (confectioner's) sugar
25 g (¾ oz/scant ¼ cup)
 cocoa powder

To serve
150 ml (5 fl oz/scant ⅔ cup)
 double (heavy)
 cream, whipped

Preheat the oven to 180°C (non-fan)/350°F/gas 4. Grease and line a 18 x 24 x 6 cm (7 x 9½ x 2½ in) baking tin (pan).

Make the cake by whisking the egg whites to soft peaks. Add the sugar and whisk until the meringue looks shiny. Mix in the egg yolks, one at a time. Sift the flour and cocoa powder on top and gently fold them into the egg mixture. Pour the batter into the tin and level with a spatula.

Bake for 20–25 minutes on the lower shelf of the oven until an inserted skewer comes out clean.

Turn the cake out onto a cooling rack and peel off the baking paper. When the cake has cooled, slice it half horizontally. You may need to trim the top if the middle has risen too much, but bear in mind that it is better to use the base layer on the top. In this way, you will have a flat surface to glaze.

To make the syrup, caramelise the sugar in a medium deep saucepan over a medium–high heat. Keep swirling the pan so that the sugar caramelises evenly. Aim to make a dark caramel, since we need some of that bitterness to come through. Carefully add the hot water, increase the heat and boil fiercely for 1 minute. Set aside to cool, then stir in the Angostura bitters.

Make the buttercream by whisking the butter until fluffy. Add the icing sugar and cocoa powder, then whisk until smooth and not grainy. Add the milk a tablespoon at a time until the cream looks spreadable.

Divide the syrup into 2 portions and drizzle evenly over each cake layer on the cut side, then sandwich the cake layers together with the buttercream. Place in the refrigerator to set.

For glaze 1: Soften the royal icing in a bowl set over a pan of boiling water. Remove from the heat and mix in the water, one spoonful at a time, to melt the icing and avoid lumps. Add the cocoa powder and combine well. You may need to add more water to bring it to the consistency of double (heavy) cream.

For glaze 2: Combine all the ingredients until smooth.

Remove the cake from the fridge, trim the edges and slice into 8 or 16 portions. Glaze each slice by placing a generous tablespoon of glaze on top, then push it down the sides. The slices don't have to be covered completely, so that the buttercream is still visible. Serve with a dollop of whipped cream.

Vanilla Mocha Cake with Bitter Walnuts

Tort de vanilie cu cremă mocha și nuci amărui

This is the cake that many Romanians associate with birthdays and is the recipe that was made in my family when I was growing up. The sponge bakes into an incredibly airy and light cake, albeit a tad dry. This is the reason we use a rum or flavoured sugar syrup to soak the layers before adding the cream. The batter and the rum syrup are typical of Romanian layered cakes. A usual filling is either chocolate, lemon or coffee buttercream, but I also know a recipe that is made with whipped butter mixed with plum jam. This recipe is the chocolate version with toasted walnuts – their slightly bitter skins offset the sweetness of the cream in the most delightful way.

Serves 8

4 medium eggs, separated
100 g (3½ oz/scant ½ cup) golden caster (superfine) sugar
2 teaspoons vanilla extract
1 teaspoon rosewater (optional)
125 g (4 oz/1 cup) plain (all-purpose) flour

For the bitter walnuts

150 g (5 oz/1¼ cups) walnuts, halves or quarters

For the rum syrup

60 ml (2 fl oz/¼ cup) water
2 tablespoons golden caster (superfine) sugar
75 ml (2½ fl oz/5 tablespoons) rum

For the buttercream

2 medium eggs
125 g (4 oz/generous ½ cup) golden caster (superfine) sugar
4 teaspoons powdered instant coffee
2 tablespoons cocoa powder
1 teaspoon vanilla bean paste
2 tablespoons rum (optional)
200 g (7 oz) unsalted butter, diced, plus extra for greasing

Preheat the oven to 180°C (non-fan)/350°F/gas 4. Grease and line the base of a 20 cm (8 in) cake tin (pan).

In a large bowl, whisk the egg whites to soft peaks. Gradually add the sugar and whisk until glossy. Add the egg yolks one at a time, then add the vanilla and rosewater, whisking after each addition. Sift and gently fold in the flour. Pour the batter into the prepared tin.

Bake for 30 minutes on a low shelf, or until an inserted skewer comes out clean. Cool in the tin, then remove. You can bake this a day before.

Toast the walnuts in a pan until they slightly darken. Remove immediately and allow to cool, then chop roughly.

To make the syrup, combine the water and sugar in a pan and bring to the boil. Boil for 5 minutes, remove from the heat and add the rum, then allow to cool. (For an adult-only cake, you can use just rum without making the syrup, in which case use 100 ml/3½ fl oz/scant ½ cup.)

For the buttercream, beat the eggs with the sugar, coffee and cocoa powder in a bowl set over a pan of simmering water until the sugar has dissolved, about 8 minutes. Remove from the heat, add the vanilla and rum, if using, and let cool slightly, whisking from time to time for about 3 minutes. Add the butter little by little, and gently mix until incorporated. Place in the refrigerator, but don't allow the cream to lose its spreadable consistency. When you are ready to assemble the cake, use an electric whisk on high speed to mix the buttercream very briefly to avoid splitting. Place it back in the fridge for a few minutes, then repeat. It should now be smooth and ready to use.

Slice the cake into 3 layers and brush the cut-sides with the rum syrup (or rum). Spread 3 tablespoons of the buttercream over the base layer and sprinkle with a third of the walnuts. Place the middle layer on top and repeat. Finish with the top layer and cover the cake entirely with the remaining buttercream and walnuts. Refrigerate until the buttercream firms up and serve with cherry liqueur or *vișinată*.

Chapter 9

Gluten–
or Dairy–
Free

The recipes in this chapter offer a gluten- or dairy-free option to end a meal on a lighter note. There is a mix of traditional recipes with urban, more modern creations, accompanied by a story about the Romanian Monarchy (see page 225), which I hope will delight and tempt you to make the parfait and sorbet desserts.

For traditional recipes, I've included sweet *alivenci* – cornmeal (polenta) cake, see page 223 – which is naturally gluten-free and taps into the culinary wisdom of the countryside to achieve a delicious cake using only farmhouse ingredients. Here, the simplicity of the recipe allows the sunny flavour of cornmeal to shine through.

Poaching fruit for compotes occupies a large part of the day when produce is in season. Later in the year, when fresh fruit is not available, these jars of compotes are used as a quick meal served with bread, as toppings to rice puddings or a dessert in themselves. The aromatics are herbs, whether wild or from the garden, such as thyme, savory, rosemary, bay leaf and chamomile.

Walnuts and hazelnuts, which grow in abundance in Romania, have a sacred symbolism and even if we don't always consider this when we use them in recipes, we love them for their complex flavour. Dried and candied fruits have always been central to our cuisine, adding not just sweetness but colour and texture too. As they have done through the rest of the book, they show up again here in the Armenian Dried Fruit Compote (page 240) and also alongside chocolate ice cream (page 238) in a recipe similar to the more familiar dessert called sundae.

You will also find the story of Casa Capșa, the famous patisserie shop in Bucharest. It is evocative of the creativity in the interwar period which saw Romania's artistic culinary achievements recognised across Europe. At home, many of these artisans became royal purveyors, and what better way to look at a country that was aligned with the vogueish lifestyle of Western Europe, than through the dishes served at the royal court. The story on page 225 explains it all.

Gluten- or Dairy-Free

Baked Cheesecake with Roasted Grapes

Pască fără aluat

A *pască* is a traditional Easter cheesecake baked in the middle of a rich brioche bread, resembling a tart. It is a very special cake and it took centre stage in my first book, being presented in all its glory. In this recipe I give you another version, gluten-free and served with roasted grapes. It is perhaps the only type of cheesecake in Romania to have its origins in a traditional dish and is not a direct import from other cuisines.

Serves 8

unsalted butter, for greasing
250g (9 oz/generous 1 cup) *brânză de vaci*, curd cheese or ricotta
250 g (9 oz/generous 1 cup) crème fraîche
3 medium eggs, separated
50 g (2 oz/¼ cup) caster (superfine) sugar
60 g (2¼ oz/½ cup) ground almonds
20 g (¾ oz/2 heaped tablespoons) golden sultanas, chopped if large
zest of 1 lemon
zest of 1 orange
2 teaspoons vanilla essence

For the grapes

250 g (9 oz) red and white grapes
2 tablespoons honey

Preheat the oven to 170°C (non-fan)/340°F/gas 3. Grease and line the base of a 20 cm (8 in) diameter cake tin that is 6 cm (2½ in) deep. Line a baking sheet with baking paper.

Place the grapes on the baking sheet and drizzle with the honey. Set aside.

Drain the cheese well before mixing in a bowl with the crème fraîche, egg yolks and sugar. Use a fork to loosen the mixture and add the rest of the ingredients, except the egg whites, combining well.

In a separate bowl, whisk the egg whites to stiff peaks, then gently fold into the cheese mixture. Pour into the prepared tin.

Place both the cake and the grapes in the oven and bake for 45 minutes, or until lightly golden on top. The sponge needs to come away from the sides of the tin and feel springy to the touch in the middle.

Remove from the oven and leave to stand for 10 minutes, then invert the cake onto a plate. Place another plate on top and quickly invert it again, so that the golden crust of the cheesecake is on top. Allow to cool completely before serving with the roasted grapes.

Gluten- or Dairy-Free

Baked Quince with Honey and Herbs

Gutui coapte

This is a gently scented dessert. In times past, quince were as popular as apples and appeared in many recipes, both sweet and savoury. Many in Romania buy them to put on the windowsill to enjoy their sweet, autumnal scent infusing the room. We also eat them raw. In this recipe, the quince is baked with herbs, spices and honey, which gently meld during cooking. Although I serve them as they are, you can add a little whipped cream, wine sauce (page 122), the Romanian clotted cream called *caimac*, ice cream or fresh curd cheese.

Serves 6

1 large quince (about 700 g/
    1 lb 9 oz whole)
2 cinnamon sticks
6 cloves
3 bay leaves
1 rosemary sprig (8–10 cm/
    3–4 in long)
3 small thyme sprigs
150 ml (5 fl oz/scant ⅔ cup)
    water or white wine
100 ml (3½ fl oz/scant ½ cup)
    honey
1 tablespoon rosewater
1 tablespoon unsalted butter

Preheat the oven to 200°C (non-fan)/400°F/gas 6.

Cut the quince into large wedges, remove the core and place in a ceramic baking dish large enough to accommodate them in one layer. Add the cinnamon sticks, spices and herbs. Combine the water with the honey and rosewater, and pour the mixture over the fruit. Dot the butter on top and cover the dish with kitchen foil.

Bake for 15–20 minutes until the quince starts to soften, then remove the foil and bake for a further 10 minutes.

Serve slightly warm accompanied by jam and whipped cream or the other suggestions mentioned in the introduction. These are also good cold, in the morning with breakfast oats.

Gluten- or Dairy-Free

Sweet
Cornmeal Cake

Alivencă dulce

The magical land of Bucovina, in northern Moldavia, is well known for its outstanding dairy farms and produce. Thick, unctuous *smântână* and *brânză*, crème fraîche and curd cheese are used generously in many recipes. This cake is a happy marriage between dairy and another staple ingredient in the region: cornmeal (polenta). It is traditionally made in two versions: one savoury and one sweet, and some recipes add various amounts of flour, oil and bicarbonate of soda (baking soda). While it is common in Moldavia to mix cornmeal with flour, I have deliberately returned to a basic, gluten-free recipe here.

Serves 8

450 ml (15 fl oz/1¾ cups) full-fat milk

80 g (3 oz/⅓ cup) golden caster (superfine) sugar

35 g (1¼ oz/1½ tablespoons) honey

125 g (4 oz/generous ¾ cup) fine cornmeal (polenta)

25 g (¾ oz/2 tablespoons) unsalted butter, plus extra for greasing

3 medium eggs, separated

300 g (10½ oz/1½ cups) *brânză de vaci*, set cottage cheese or ricotta

To serve

125 g (4 oz/½ cup) crème fraîche

honey, for drizzling

Bring the milk to the boil in a large pan, then reduce the heat to medium and add the sugar, honey and cornmeal. Simmer for 10 minutes until the milk has been absorbed, then stir in the butter and set aside to cool.

Butter a 15 x 22 cm (6 x 8¾ in) rectangular ceramic pie dish. Preheat the oven to 180°C (non-fan)/350°F/gas 4.

In a bowl, beat the egg whites to stiff peaks.

When the cornmeal mixture has cooled, add the egg yolks and cheese, then fold in the egg whites. Pour the mixture into the prepared dish.

Bake for 50 minutes, covering the top with kitchen foil if it cooks too quickly or reducing the heat to 170°C/340°F/gas 3. The cake will puff up and crack around the edges. Turn the oven off (even if the cake still has a slight wobble in the middle) and allow the cake to cool in the oven until just slightly warm.

When cooled, slice in the tray and serve slightly warm with crème fraîche and a drizzle of honey. It is also good cold.

Gluten- or Dairy-Free

At the Table with Romanian Royalty

✗ ✗ ✗ ✗ ✗ ✗ ✗ ✗ ✗ ✗ ✗ ✗ ✗ ✗ ✗ ✗ ✗ ✗ ✗

We haven't had a monarchy since 1947, but Romanian royalty and their lifestyles still fascinate many people.

Prince Karl of Hohenzollern-Sigmaringen was invited in 1866 to be the first prince of the newly united Wallachia and Moldovian principalities. He was later crowned as King Carol I. Known for his disciplined and calculated manner, he was a powerful and brilliant figure who quickly put Romania on the path of modernisation and progress. The focus of his reign was to achieve and maintain international recognition for the independent state and to reinforce the principle of monarchy. It was during this time that many imposing buildings were designed in a bold, eclectic architectural style and important improvements to the country's infrastructure were made, including the longest bridge over the Danube in Europe. The King's personal project started when he fell in love with the breathtaking beauty of the Carpathian mountains. In the mountain resort of Sinaia, he built his summer residence, Peleş Castle, in a style that combined Italian elegance with German artistic elements.

Historian Ştefania Dinu wrote in her book about royal etiquette, *Mese şi meniuri regale*, that Carol I organised his eating hours with the accuracy of a military operation: 6am breakfast, lunch at 12pm (or 1pm on holiday), 5pm afternoon tea and 8pm dinner. The routine menus were strikingly frugal, the ambience extremely formal and the allocated time very short. It is said that he loved fish and it was in the Danube Delta that he first had fish *borş* and carp. He loved Romanian Azuga beer and Drăgăşani wines. The desserts were almost an afterthought, even at important dinners and festivities. Very often there was fresh or poached fruit in the style of *macédoine*, sorbet and ice creams, a dish of rice pudding with apricots called *Abricots à la Conde* (a similar dish is on page 122), and very rarely there might have been a cake.

His nephew, Ferdinand I, inherited the crown in 1914 and was nicknamed 'The Unifier', since it was under his rule that Transylvania joined Romania. Ferdinand I married Princess Maria Alexandra Victoria, who was Queen Victoria's granddaughter from her second son Prince Alfred, Duke of Edinburgh. Queen Marie of Romania disliked the austere atmosphere at the court and never adjusted to it. The country continued its architectural transformation. The Queen designed and directly supervised the improvements of a second royal residence in the capital, Cotroceni Palace, the century-old residence of many rulers before the monarchy, which was completed with central heating and a gymnastic hall.

Not surprisingly, Queen Marie changed the table habits and served breakfast at 9am or even at 10am. Her husband preferred to have his main meal of the day in the morning, with eggs cooked in three ways, grilled beef steak and veal schnitzel with steamed potatoes, followed by toast with honey and fruit. Official dinners were less formal and full of laughter and entertainment. However, dessert menus were just as frugal, although cheese made an appearance served with fruit, and also the 'unmissable' chocolate bonbons from Casa Capşa (see why on page 239). Almost every menu ended with

Gluten- or Dairy-Free

coffee, which would have been provided by Avedis Carabelaian, a famous Armenian coffee merchant and royal purveyor. Queen Marie was the first one to encourage her chefs to serve traditional Romanian food and give Romanian names to dishes. This trend continued at the court of her son, King Carol II, where we saw stuffed cabbage rolls with cornmeal bread and sour cream or smoked pork ribs with butterbean stew. Most of the ingredients were produced at local farms and very few were brought in from abroad. Dessert menus included cheese tarts, honeycomb or bavarois cream, alongside the regular ice creams, parfaits and fresh fruit.

Carol II loved entertainment. He was an unconventional king, having renounced the Crown and divorced his wife, Princess Helena of Greece and Denmark, to live with his mistress who was a socialite. The difficult situation just before the Second World War forced parliament to recall the King, but unfortunately Carol II had to abdicate, allowing a military dictatorship to align Romania with Nazi Germany. After a coup d'état four years later, his son King Mihai I returned to the throne and steered the country away from the dictatorship, influencing the outcome of the war in Eastern Europe. Sadly, it was too late and the monarchy in Romania was ended by Russian control and Communist regime in 1948.

The communists arrested everyone who worked for the royal household and sent them to forced labour camps or, depending on what ethnicity they were, straight to Russia. It was here that, unknown to the new party members, an extraordinary story began.

A French president in Bucharest

The French President de Gaulle took the historic decision to visit Bucharest in 1968, when the country lived under the purest communist dogma, although worse was still to come. This sent shivers down the spine of the politicians who realised that they didn't have a chef to cook for the occasion. The only one up to the task was the former Royal Head Chef, who had been sent to a workers' canteen in the middle of nowhere when the King abdicated 20 years earlier. Having tracked him down, the communists drove Iosif Strasman straight to the French Embassy where he recreated his sophisticated royal menus for the important two-day event. He later refused the discreet offer of the Ambassador to join the French delegation back to Paris, on the basis that his roots were in Romania.

In 1980, in an unexpected move on the part of the Communist regime, he was allowed to publish his own cookery book, full of sophisticated dishes that nobody had ever heard of. It was a time when stores were empty and food was scarce. It must have felt like reading culinary science fiction, but the regime had always been eager to prove that the communist proletariat had access to the most sophisticated luxuries, if only in its imagination.

Today, some of the royal family have returned to Romania and one of King Mihai's daughters, Princess Margareta of Romania, is the current custodian of the Crown. I hope that at official dinners ice creams are still popular. On the next few pages, I have given you two recipes inspired by Iosif Strasman and his royal menus.

Apricot and Mint Sorbet

Sorbet de caise cu mentă

✕ ✕ ✕ ✕ ✕ ✕ ✕ ✕ ✕ ✕ ✕ ✕ ✕ ✕ ✕ ✕ ✕ ✕ ✕

A sorbet is the ideal dessert to enjoy the pure flavour of fruit
on a hot summer's day. I am pairing the apricot with mint,
which adds a hint of refreshing sharpness.

Serves 4

300 ml (10 fl oz/1¼ cups)
  water
300 g (10½ oz/1⅓ cups)
  golden caster
  (superfine) sugar
1 kg (2 lb 4 oz) apricots, sliced
zest and juice of 1 large lemon
4 large mint leaves, chopped,
  plus extra to garnish
1 tablespoon almond extract

In a large pan, bring the water and sugar to the boil and simmer until the sugar has dissolved. Add the apricots, lemon zest and juice, and cook together for 5 minutes. Remove from the heat, add the mint and almond extract, and allow to cool completely.

Transfer to a food processor and blend until smooth, then pass through a sieve (fine strainer) into a bowl, pressing down on the fruit pulp to extract as much juice as possible.

If you have an ice-cream machine, you can churn the mixture according to the manufacturer's instructions.

If you don't have an ice-cream machine, pour the sorbet into a cake tin or plastic container and place it in the freezer for about 1 hour, or until the edges start to turn icy.

Remove from the freezer and whisk or blend in a food processor once more, then return to the freezer for a further 30 minutes.

Repeat the whisking/blending process one final time, then freeze the sorbet until needed.

Blend again before serving topped with mint sprigs.

Gluten- or Dairy-Free

Coffee Parfait with Dark Chocolate

Parfait de cafea cu ciocolată neagră

✖ ✖ ✖ ✖ ✖ ✖ ✖ ✖ ✖ ✖ ✖ ✖ ✖ ✖ ✖ ✖ ✖ ✖

This is an elegant dessert that relies on the energising powers of coffee and chocolate to liven up the mood. It is creamy and very rich, and therefore best served in small quantities.

Serves 4

2 tablespoons powdered instant coffee

80 ml (2½ fl oz/5 tablespoons) just-boiled water

4 large eggs, yolks only

50 g (2 oz/¼ cup) golden caster (superfine) sugar

50 ml (1¾ fl oz/3 tablespoons) coffee liqueur (or orange liqueur for a different flavour)

200 ml (7 fl oz/scant 1 cup) double (heavy) cream

50 g (2 oz) dark chocolate

Combine the instant coffee with the water and stir well until it dissolves. If you have a coffee machine, you can make a 80 ml (2½ fl oz) very strong espresso.

Whisk the egg yolks with the sugar in a heatproof bowl, then place it over a pan of simmering water. Add the instant coffee and whisk until thick and smooth. Take off the heat and keep whisking until it cools a little, add the coffee liqueur and place in the refrigerator to cool completely.

Add the double cream and whisk it into the sabayon, preferably with a handheld mixer.

Line an 18 cm (7 in) cake tin (pan) with clingfilm (plastic wrap) and pour in the mixture. Freeze until needed.

To serve, remove from the tin and allow to soften slightly. Grate dark chocolate on top, then slice into wedges and serve.

Gluten- or Dairy-Free

Îles Flotantes with Caramel Walnut Praline

Lapte de pasăre

There are two ways to prepare a floating island, both of which give similar results. One is to poach the meringues in milk and place them on a delicate, thin crème anglaise, while the other calls for the meringue to be baked and the crème poured around it. The one we made at home was baked in one large dish, then mum would scoop out the meringue to divide it between us. We called it *lapte de pasăre*, 'bird's milk'. I've chosen to make a *griliaș* or *kranz*, a walnut praline, as it is one of the most popular decorations added to cakes and desserts in Romania, but feel free to skip this step if you wish to keep things simple.

Makes 6

For the walnut praline
100 g (3½ oz/scant ½ cup)
   caster (superfine) sugar
100 g (3½ oz/scant 1 cup)
   walnuts

For the crème anglaise
3 medium eggs, separated
25 g (1¾ oz/2 tablespoons)
   caster (superfine) sugar
1 teaspoon plain
   (all-purpose) flour
300 ml (10 fl oz/1¼ cups)
   full-fat milk
2 teaspoons vanilla bean paste

For the îles flotantes
unsalted butter, for greasing
180 g (6½ oz/generous ¾ cup)
   caster (superfine) sugar,
   plus extra for dusting
(3 egg whites from the
   eggs above)

Make the walnut praline by melting the sugar in a small pan over a medium heat. Swirl the pan every now and then, to melt the sugar evenly without burning. When it starts to turn golden, quickly mix in the walnuts. Transfer the mixture to a baking sheet lined with non-stick paper or a silicone liner and spread in an even layer, not necessarily the size of the sheet. Set aside to cool.

When the praline is cool, break it into pieces and blitz to a coarse texture in a food processor. Set aside.

Make the crème anglaise by whisking together the egg yolks in a large bowl with the sugar and flour. Heat the milk in a saucepan and simmer for a couple of minutes, then gradually pour the milk over the egg yolk mixture, whisking all the time. Transfer the mixture back to the pan and simmer over a medium heat until it starts to thicken. It needs to have the consistency of single (light) cream. Remove from the heat, add the vanilla, cover and set aside.

Preheat the oven to 140°C (non-fan)/275°F/gas ½. Lightly butter the inside of a baking dish, about 18 cm (7 in) in diameter and at least 6 cm (2½ in) deep, then coat it with caster sugar.

In a clean bowl, whisk the egg whites to soft peaks, then gradually add the sugar, whisking to a glossy, thick consistency and until the sugar is dissolved. Spoon the meringue into the prepared dish.

Bake for 30 minutes on a lower shelf of the oven until the top looks dry and crisp.

Serve warm, scooping the meringue into bowls and pouring the crème anglaise around. Sprinkle the walnut praline on top.

Gluten- or Dairy-Free

Note

If you have any walnut praline left over, store it in an airtight container and use it to top ice creams or mousses.

Chestnut Cream

Cremă de castane

This recipe comes from Transylvania, where according to many people, including my family, the chestnut purée is the best in the country. Delicately sweet, perfumed with vanilla and with a hint of rum, I remember how I loved eating it straight from the jar, without adding the cream. For this recipe, I also tried a version with Maraschino liqueur, since I adore its wonderful cherry flavour, and it makes a good alternative to rum, even if a little sweet.

Serves 6

3 tablespoons water
80 g (3 oz/⅓ cup) caster (superfine) sugar
500 g (1 lb 2 oz) ready-to-eat chestnuts
25 ml (scant 2 tablespoons) dark rum (or Maraschino liqueur for an alternative flavour)
2 teaspoons vanilla bean paste
125 ml (4 fl oz/½ cup) double (heavy) cream
cherry jam or grated dark chocolate, to serve (optional)

Bring the water and sugar to the boil in a small pan, then cook for 5–8 minutes until the syrup thickens slightly.

Blitz the chestnuts to a rough paste in a food processor. With the motor running on low speed, add the sugar syrup, rum or Maraschino and the vanilla. Mix until smooth but not silky. Transfer the mixture to a bowl and place in the refrigerator.

In a separate bowl, whisk the cream to soft peaks. Fold 2 tablespoons of the whipped cream into the chestnut cream.

Serve in small glasses or bowls, topped with the remaining cream and, if you wish, with a teaspoonful of cherry jam or a little grated dark chocolate.

Gluten- or Dairy-Free

Mill Wheels – Mini Chocolate and Hazelnut Meringues

Bezele roți de moară

This elegant dessert became known as 'mill wheels' in Romania, being much larger than the ones in this recipe. They know different variations throughout the country, having originally travelled from Denmark, where they were created in celebration of the famous actress Sarah Bernhardt. She also visited Romania, performing at different theatres including one in Brăila, which was at the time a prosperous port on the Danube river.

Makes 12

2 egg whites
145 g (5 oz/⅔ cup) caster (superfine) sugar
1 teaspoon lemon juice

For the filling and decoration

50 ml (1¾ oz/3 tablespoons) double (heavy) cream
50 g (2 oz) dark chocolate (70–85% cocoa solids)
20 g (¾ oz) blanched, roasted hazelnuts, finely chopped

Preheat the oven to 140°C (non-fan)/275°F/gas ½. Line a baking sheet with baking paper.

In a large bowl, whisk the egg whites to soft peaks, then gradually add the sugar and lemon juice until the meringue forms very stiff peaks and the sugar has dissolved. Transfer to a piping bag fitted with a medium (1 cm/½ in) nozzle and pipe 24 meringues of equal size onto the baking sheet. When piping, keep the nozzle 2 mm (⅟₁₆ in) above the baking paper, without swirling, lifting slightly to create height. Make them about 3.5 cm (1½ in) in diameter. Dip one finger in cold water and gently tuck in any peaks that are sticking out.

Bake for 40 minutes, then turn the heat off and allow the meringues to cool in the oven for a few minutes with the door left ajar. Transfer to a cooling rack.

Make the filling by heating the cream in a small saucepan. Chop the chocolate finely, place in a bowl and pour the hot cream on top. Stir well until it looks glossy.

Sandwich together two meringues with a little chocolate, then sprinkle some finely chopped hazelnuts on the outside of the filling. Place on a pretty plate and serve.

Gluten- or Dairy-Free

Fruit Cocktail with Chocolate Ice Cream and Whipped Cream

Coupe Jacques

In the interwar period in Romania, restaurants and cookbooks were importing a lot of fashionable dishes from the West. A particular category of desserts proved to be quite popular: 'coupes' as in 'desserts served in glass bowls'. Made with fruit, whether fresh, candied or from a compote, they were topped with whipped cream, ice cream and a dash of alcohol. In this recipe for Coupe Jacques, the key ingredient is the perfumed, gooey and sweet orange peel. It is important to use very good quality peel, or make your own since it is not very complicated. The glamour of Coupe Jacques would have relied on the luxurious Champagne poured over the fruit, a touch that sadly was lost over the years. You can use another bubbly drink, but if you don't fancy it, use orange liqueur and rum.

Serves 4

175 g (6 oz) mixed dried
   fruit (apples, pears,
   apricots, plums)
50 g (2 oz) dried cherries
60 g (2¼ oz) diced candied
   orange peel (see page 264),
   plus a little extra
   to decorate
2 tablespoons rum
2 tablespoons orange liqueur
zest and juice of 1 orange
1 tablespoon orange
   blossom water
60 ml (2 fl oz/¼ cup) double
   (heavy) cream
1 teaspoon icing
   (confectioner's) sugar
1 teaspoon vanilla bean paste
100 g (3½ oz) good-quality
   dark chocolate ice cream

In a bowl, mix all the dried fruit and orange peel with the rum, orange liqueur, orange zest and juice, and orange blossom water. Leave to soak for at least 1 hour.

In a separate bowl, whisk the cream with the icing sugar and vanilla until the peaks hold their shape.

Assemble the dish by placing a couple of tablespoons of the dried fruit compote together with some of the soaking liquor in a shallow bowl. Add some candied orange peel, and top with a scoop of chocolate ice cream and the whipped cream. Scatter a little more candied orange peel on top and serve immediately.

Gluten- or Dairy-Free

Chocolate Mousse with Orange Marmalade

Crema de ciocolată cu marmeladă de portocale Capșa

Casa Capșa is a historic pastry shop, café and restaurant in Bucharest, founded in 1852. Their gilded halls attracted aristocracy, politicians, writers, artists and journalists, who met here to eat the best cakes, chocolates and ice creams in this part of Europe. In 1873, Capșa received the Grand Medal at Vienna World's Fair, becoming internationally renowned and appointed a Royal Warrant by both Prince Milan Obrenović of Serbia and Prince Ferdinand of Bulgaria. Of course, Capșa also supplied the Romanian royal household with chocolate bonbons and truffles. The unparalleled repertoire and skills of the pastry chefs made the transition between the Middle Eastern world of desserts (which dominated our cuisine up to the 20th century) to French-style chocolates and mousses. In this recipe, I give you a personal interpretation of one of their famous chocolate desserts.

Serves 4

280 ml (9½ fl oz/scant 1¼ cups) double (heavy) cream
120 g (4 oz) dark chocolate (at least 75% cocoa solids), chopped
1 teaspoon cocoa powder, plus extra to decorate
80 g (3 oz) fine-cut orange marmalade, plus extra to decorate

Heat the cream in a milk pan, stirring from time to time to avoid burning.

Place the chopped chocolate in a heatproof bowl, pour over the hot cream and allow to melt for 1 minute. Whisk the mixture together with the cocoa powder to a smooth consistency and place in the refrigerator to cool completely.

When cold, add the marmalade and use an electric whisk to whip the chocolate cream to an airy consistency.

Spoon into glass bowls, place 1 teaspoonful of orange marmalade on top of each portion and dust with a little cocoa powder. Serve immediately.

Gluten- or Dairy-Free

Armenian Dried Fruit Compote with Walnuts

Compot Armenesc

This compote is a very good way to serve dried fruit when nothing else is in season. It is a versatile recipe that can be adapted to your preference, using your favourite fruit. Although it is traditionally served by itself, it can be accompanied by yoghurt or whipped cream, or served alongside set creams or ice creams.

Serves 4

500 ml (17 fl oz/2 cups) water
4 teaspoons loose tea
  (try linden, chamomile,
  elderflower, jasmine
  or green)
100 g (3½ oz/½ cup) prunes,
  chopped
100 g (3½ oz/generous ½ cup)
  dried apricots, chopped
50 g (2 oz/¼ cup) dried
  pears, chopped
50 g (2 oz/scant ½ cup)
  dried cherries
100 g (3½ oz/generous ¾ cup)
  golden raisins (sultanas)
80 g (3 oz/¾ cup) walnuts,
  roughly chopped
2 tablespoons honey
1 tablespoon rosewater
1 vanilla pod
1 cinnamon stick
zest of 1 large orange

Bring the water to the boil, add the tea leaves and simmer for 5 minutes. Turn the heat off and cover the pan with a plate.

Combine the rest of the ingredients in a bowl, then strain the hot liquid over them. Stir and leave to soak for at least 2 hours before serving.

Store in a covered bowl or in a jar in the fridge and eat within a couple of days.

Chapter 10

Sweet Snacks and Gifts

Homemade, edible gifts are a wonderful thing to offer to family and friends, and the recipes in this chapter represent a collection of snacks and treats that I grew up with in Romania. Although snacking is not really a habit that we have in our culture, during Lent it sees us through the day, and some recipes here are used only on such occasions. We eat *halva* (see page 248) made with sunflower seeds, which are more or less a product of the flourishing sunflower oil industry. The sweet sesame bars (see page 251) are also popular, even beyond Lent days, and are almost always bought rather than made at home.

This chapter also includes a recipe for truffles called 'potatoes' (see page 246) – apart from their looks, they have no connection to either chocolate ganache or the starchy vegetable. Their powdered exterior was often achieved with carob rather than cocoa powder, since the latter was not always available in stores. Homemade chocolate, as in a sort of fudge, was something we all preferred to eat when I was little, when most of the chocolate on the market was imported from China.

There is also a recipe for *halviță* in the form of a layered confection, which at home was called *Lica*, a replacement of the German name *Karlsbad*, perhaps named after a local commercial bakery. I chose to balance its sweetness with wild fennel seeds, an ingredient that I found in Romanian cookery books of the 19th century. It works well and avoids the need to add dried fruit or lemon zest, whose acidity doesn't always work in desserts.

Last but not least come the jams, confitures and candied citrus peel recipes, which can easily be gifts since there is nothing better than to give something that you put so much love into. Their importance in Romanian cuisine is seen in our habit of serving them on their own, alongside a small cup of strong coffee and a glass of water. They make for a dessert in themselves. Having baked your way through this book, you will have noticed by now how often we use jam in desserts of all kinds, to add a natural flavour and colour, but also to mediate between two different layers of texture. So, sending someone a jar of jam can be an invitation to explore Romanian cuisine in more than one way.

I hope that you will enjoy the revival of these recipes and share them with the people around you.

Sweet Snacks and Gifts

Fig and Carob 'Potatoes'

Cartofi cu smochine și roșcove

These fig truffles take their name from their resemblance to potatoes.
The carob, although often used to make up for the lack of cocoa powder,
has a subtle nutty flavour, and is more perfumed. It also makes a wonderful
alternative to hot chocolate.

Makes 14

150 g (5 oz/¾ cup) dried
  figs, chopped
fruit juice, warmed, for soaking
  (optional)
200 g (7 oz) shortbread
  biscuits (cookies)
50 g (2 oz/⅓ cup)
  hazelnuts, chopped
50 g (2 oz/⅓ cup)
  almonds, chopped
5 tablespoons full-fat milk
50 g (2 oz/¼ cup) caster
  (superfine) sugar
80 g (3 oz) unsalted butter
30 g (1 oz/¼ cup)
  carob powder

For dusting

20 g (¾ oz/3 tablespoons)
  carob powder

Put the chopped figs in a bowl and cover with boiling water (or warm
fruit juice, if you like).

Put the shortbread biscuits in a sealable bag and crush them with
a rolling pin.

Drain and squeeze the liquid from the figs, then place them back
in a bowl and add the crushed shortbread and chopped nuts.

In a small pan, bring the milk, sugar and butter to the boil. Stir in the
carob powder and cook for 2 minutes. Pour the mixture over the dry
ingredients and combine well, then place the bowl in the refrigerator
for 1 hour.

Spread the carob powder for dusting over a large plate. Use a tablespoon
to scoop up some of the mixture, then roll it in the carob powder. Use
your hands to form the truffle into an oval shape and press it gently on
top. Set aside on a different plate. Work quickly, then place the truffles
in the refrigerator for a few hours to firm up.

Store, covered, in the refrigerator for up to 3 days.

Sunflower-Seed Halva

Halva cu seminţe de floarea soarelui

This is a very popular snack in Romania, especially during the days of Lent when we are hardly allowed to eat anything. It is usually store-bought, but I wanted to rediscover this flavour of my childhood and adulthood, especially now that I live in the UK, so here is a homemade version. My grandmother and I loved to eat this halva with bread, to appease our hunger. It is good for breaking fast while still observing Lent.

Makes 2 small loaves

300 g (10½ oz/2½ cups) sunflower seeds
60 g (2¼ oz/generous ¼ cup) golden caster (superfine) sugar
1 tablespoon instant coffee powder (optional)
100 g (3½ oz) unsalted butter, melted
2 tablespoons runny honey

Lightly toast the sunflower seeds in a dry frying pan (skillet), stirring constantly. Leave to cool completely.

Transfer the toasted seeds to a food processor and blitz together with the sugar and coffe, if using, to a fine powder. Transfer to a bowl.

Combine the melted butter with the honey, then pour it over the seeds. Use a spoon to mix the ingredients, as you only need to stir them a few times, until the butter is absorbed. If you stir it too much or do this step in the food processor, the butter will start to seep out and your halva will become greasy.

Spoon the halva into two 12 x 10 cm (5 x 4 in) foil trays and press it with the back of the spoon to even the top. Wrap in clingfilm (plastic wrap) and place in the refrigerator overnight to set.

When you are ready to serve, remove from the tins and cut into thick slices. Store, covered, in the refrigerator.

Sesame and Thyme Honey Bars

Batoane de susan cu miere și cimbru

This is an excellent treat for when you need a little energy. I used to eat it at school during breaks, but now I mostly make it during Lent. When you add the thyme, the aromas in the kitchen change instantly from sweet to pepper-spicy. This is delicious not just as a power snack but also to accompany ice creams or soft desserts.

Makes 8–10

250 g (9 oz/1⅔ cups)
   sesame seeds
250 ml (8½ fl oz/1 cup) honey
zest of 1 lemon
2 tablespoons fresh thyme
   or winter savory, chopped
unsalted butter, for greasing

Preheat the oven to 180°C (non-fan)/350°F/gas 4. Line a baking sheet with baking paper.

Spread the sesame seeds over the baking sheet and roast in the oven until golden, about 20 minutes. Keep a close eye on them, as they can burn really quickly.

Meanwhile, bring the honey to the boil in a pan until foamy. Add the hot sesame seeds, lemon zest and thyme, then reduce the heat to medium and keep cooking for a few more minutes, stirring constantly, until the honey starts to change colour.

Carefully spread the mixture in a thin layer over a large sheet of baking paper. Place another sheet of baking paper on top and use a rolling pin to spread the paste evenly until about 4 mm (¼ in) thick. Remove the paper on top and leave to cool for 10 minutes.

Lightly grease the blade of a knife by pulling it through a piece of butter, then cut the sesame mixture into bars. Allow to cool completely and store in an airtight container for up to 5 days with pieces of baking paper in between to stop them sticking together.

Sweet Snacks and Gifts

Homemade Fudge
with Dried Cherries

Ciocolată de casă cu vișine uscate

This is a nostalgic chocolate treat, closer in texture to fudge than to chocolate. The key flavour is the milk powder, which you can find in health or international food stores, especially the organic version. I have tried many traditional recipes and most of them require a sugar thermometer, otherwise it is hard to reach the right consistency. Because of that, I often ended up with caramels! The method in this recipe is an easier compromise and works just as well.

Makes 16 thin wedges

200 g (7 oz/2 cups)
 organic milk powder
 (*not* baby milk powder)
2 tablespoons cocoa powder
120 ml (4 fl oz/½ cup) water
30 g (1 oz) unsalted butter
50 ml (2 fl oz/3 tablespoons)
 honey
80 g (3 oz/generous ½ cup)
 hazelnuts, chopped
80 g (3 oz/⅔ cup)
 dried cherries

Line a small round dish, about 18 cm (7 in) in diameter, with clingfilm (plastic wrap).

Mix the milk powder with the cocoa powder in a bowl.

In a small pan, bring the water, butter and honey to the boil, then cook for a further 2–3 minutes. Pour the mixture over the milk and cocoa powder and stir well to combine, then add the hazelnuts and cherries. Pour the mixture into the prepared dish and spread evenly, then cover and place in the refrigerator overnight.

The next day, cut into wedges. Store, covered, in the refrigerator.

Honey Nougat with Walnuts and Wild Fennel Seeds

Halviță cu nucă și semințe de angelica

The herby, aniseed aroma of the angelica (wild fennel) seeds here counteract the sweetness of *halviță*, which is a kind of nougat, but it's still so rich that it can only be enjoyed in small slices. My mum would use this method, taken from a Romanian cookery book, *Sanda Marin* – one that almost every Romanian had in their kitchen. The wafers can be sourced from International or Eastern European food stores or online – they are sometimes called plain tort waffle or wafer sheets.

Makes 8 large slices

2 sheets of Karlsbad or Lica wafers or rice wafer sheets
120 g (4 oz/1 cup) walnuts, roughly chopped
30 g (1 oz/¼ cup) wild fennel seeds
3 egg whites
150 ml (5 fl oz/scant ⅔ cup) honey
150 g (5 oz/⅔ cup) caster (superfine) sugar
juice of ½ lemon
1 teaspoon almond extract

Line a 20 x 30 x 2 cm (8 x 12 x ¾ in) baking tray (pan), with a large piece of clingfilm (plastic wrap), so it hangs over the edges. Trim both wafer sheets so they will fit perfectly inside the tray, then place one wafer sheet inside the tray.

Lightly toast the walnuts and fennel seeds together in a dry pan, then set aside.

Bring a pan of water to the boil. In a large, heatproof bowl, whisk the egg whites to soft peaks, then gradually add the honey, sugar and lemon juice. Place the bowl on top the pan of boiling water and keep whisking until it thickens to almost a paste consistency that is coming away from the base of the bowl – this takes about 45 minutes. Add the almond extract towards the end of cooking so that it does not lose flavour. When it is ready, add the nuts and fennel seeds, and combine well.

Working quickly, pour the mixture on top of the wafer sheet, cover with the second wafer, pressing slightly, and wrap with the overhanging clingfilm. Leave to set overnight.

When set, it will still have a soft consistency. Remove from the tray and clingfilm, slice and enjoy.

Sweet Snacks and Gifts

Jewish Merchants in Eastern Romania

xxxxxxxx • xxxxxxxxxx • x xx

'It seems more urgent and effective to me to achieve a harmony in my own life between the Romanian and Jewish parts of my character than to obtain or lose certain civil rights. I would like to know, for instance, what anti-Semitic law could erase from my being the irrevocable fact of having been born by the Danube and loving that place,' wrote Mihail Sebastian in his novel *For Two Thousand Years*. Behind the pen name, he was Iosif Mendel Hechter, a controversial figure during the interwar period, being seen by his own Jewish community as a defector, and by the right-wing intellectuals as ultra-nationalistic.

During the Communist regime, his theatre plays were often adapted for TV or radio – romantic, playful, bittersweet love stories surrounded by an urban society full of vanities or a gossipy, prejudiced rural life. After the fall of the regime, two of his political memoirs made their way onto the shelves of bookstores, and it became obvious that whatever else he wrote was meant to keep him away from what was going on around him: the unleashed anti-Semitic society of the mid-20th century, the pogroms and the suffering. Intellectuals, many of whom were his own friends, incited violence, masterminded the tragic events and delivered lectures in universities attended by hundreds of people.

Sebastian was born in Brăila, which at that time was an important port on the Danube in eastern Romania. It was a town with an eye on French fashion, where people attended soirées and music concerts, organised balls and went to the local theatre, where once even Sarah Bernhardt came to perform. By then, the city had witnessed at least two centuries of flourishing commerce, being one of the only three ports on the Danube to trade with the Ottoman Empire at the beginning of the 19th century. It would also have been the port of call for merchants covering the route that connected Poland in the north to trade hubs on the Danube and the Black Sea in the south-east in Romania. In large cities, such as Botoșani, Suceava and Iași, Jewish quarters grew busy and wealthy creating a constellation of market towns where Jewish traders in particular would have stopped at inns or stayed with relatives. It was a powerful network. It is said that the direct business with Poland bothered the Ottoman Empire, which – at least in theory – considered itself to have exclusive access to the vast amounts of honey, salted meat, wax and cow hides coming from Moldavia.

Jews settled in eastern and south-eastern Romania at various times, starting in the 9th century, mostly fleeing persecution or migrating from Poland and Russia. They came to establish flourishing communities as different Moldavian princes encouraged them to stay in order to boost the urban economy of the region. The fact that they were not allowed to own land explained the predilection for living in towns, where they were craftsmen, merchants and shopkeepers. They processed leather and made boots, kept shops as tailors, jewellery and bookbinders, and also butchers, grocers and bakers. It is interesting that stores selling alcoholic spirits were almost entirely in their hands and, of course, they were allowed to sell kosher wines. In Botoșani, at the northern tip of Moldavia, 75 per cent of the merchants and 68 per cent of the craftsmen were Jewish. The numbers were similar all the

Sweet Snacks and Gifts

way to the Danube in the south. Many also operated in the business of lending money and renting buildings, triggering an infamous reputation and the dreadful nickname 'Jewish rent' for any payment of this kind, regardless of the ethnicity of the landlord.

Princes often recognised the Jewish contribution to a flourishing economy by granting them the rights to trade and different tax exemptions, even if often these freedoms were denied again, because of pressure from other guilds or social structures. The most important of all was a fixed annual tax, that the whole community had to pay, which allowed the rich to pay the fees for the poor, helping each other out through difficult times. Another accepted rule within the community was that kosher butchers would sell the meat at a slightly higher price, the difference going as payment for the Jewish teacher and towards other costs for education. Parents were committed to offering their children a chance for a better life, which would have also allowed them to keep the Jewish religion and identity alive.

It is from this intricate history that the Jewish cuisine took shape and absorbed the influences around it. Moldavia had one of the largest Yiddish-speaking communities, while the Sephardic Jews from Istanbul were the last to settle here and were usually richer. The German influence in baking is visible, with *kugel*, a yeasted cake, or *kindli*, a version of shortcrust strudel, and matzo dumplings; for the well-to-do, *flondi* and *Sacher torte*.

While I was writing about the cuisine, trying to see which dishes were Jewish and which Romanian, I had Mihail Sebastian's thoughts lingering in my mind. My quest turned to finding those recipes that were particular to Romania, and it became hard not to notice how influential the Jewish cuisine was on what today we call Romanian dishes: noodle puddings, fritters and jam crescents. As usual, influences travel back and forth both ways, hence I have encountered a variety of dishes identifying as Jewish using cornmeal (polenta), including the sweet cornmeal mush served with *magiun* (plum jam), or the dumplings called *papanași*, and the lavish use of yoghurt and garlic. *Pască* is a source of confusion, meaning *matzo* for Jewish cooks and a cheese-filled brioche cake for Romanians. What stood out of many recipes was *humântaș*, the triangular cookies filled with jam or walnuts and baked for Purim, which are still prepared in Romania.

Today, I feel that in Romania we have lost the richness of this community, whether through war, migration or assimilation. In the few people I talked to, I could see that perhaps the strict dietary rules are more relaxed, although one can only be kosher or not. Some people eat *Salam de Sibiu*, our famous pork salami, or ask their relatives to send it to them in Israel. Others celebrate only the main festivals or the ones they like the most. Meanwhile, non-Jews are learning about and acknowledging the past, and this kind of acceptance builds something new and with a better future. Local Jewish events are enthusiastically attended by non-Jews too, breaking barriers built through political propaganda and a biased history.

Jewish Cookies with Plum Butter

Humântaș evreiesc cu magiun de prune

✕ ✕ ✕ ✕ ✕ ✕ ✕ ✕ ✕ ✕ ✕ ✕ ✕ ✕ ✕ ✕ ✕ ✕

There are many variations of these Jewish cookies around the world. My friend Katia's family in Bucharest make them with *magiun*, plum butter. She told me to seal the cookies at the top, as opposed to leaving the centres open, since they are easier to bake in this way. Although I found recipes using butter, oil is considered traditional since it's kosher, so the cookies can be served after meat dishes. Real plum butter takes a while to make, so this is a quick way to prepare it at home. Even if it is not the traditional method, the filling has the right consistency for the task, and the cookies are tasty and slightly tangy in the middle.

Makes 20

For the dough
1 large egg
50 g (2 oz/¼ cup) golden caster (supefine) sugar
3 tablespoons sunflower oil
220 g (8 oz/1¾ cups) plain (all-purpose) flour, plus extra for dusting
½ teaspoon baking powder
2 tablespoons cold water

For the filling
120 g (4 oz/generous ½ cup) prunes
50 g (2 oz/½ cup) walnuts
2 tablespoons lemon juice

To finish
1 egg, beaten, for brushing icing (confectioner's) sugar, for dusting

First, make the dough. In a bowl, mix together the egg, sugar and oil. Add the rest of the ingredients and knead to a smooth dough. Wrap and place in the refrigerator for 30 minutes.

To make the filling, blitz the prunes, nuts and lemon juice in a food processor to form a paste with a firm consistency.

Preheat the oven to 180°C (non-fan)/350°F/gas 4. Line a baking sheet with baking paper.

Flour the work surface and roll out the dough to 3 mm (⅛ in) thick. Cut out circles of dough with an 8 cm (3 in) cookie cutter.

Take one circle of dough and brush the edges with a little beaten egg. Add 7-10 g (¼-½ oz) of the prune filling in the middle. Pinch two sides together to form the tip of a triangle at the top, then pinch the other two lateral ones to form the triangle base. Press the sides around the filling and up to close at the top (if you like, you can leave the centres open in the middle for a more traditional look). Place on the baking sheet and brush lightly with beaten egg. Repeat with the remaining circles of dough and filling. If the dough is getting too soft, place in the refrigerator again until firm.

Bake for 10-12 minutes until lightly golden.

Allow to cool, then dust with icing sugar and serve.

Jams and Confitures

There are many types of fruit preserves that we love to prepare in Romania, with jams and confitures being the most popular. Jam is when you cook the fruit and sugar together at the same time, allowing it to reach the desired consistency. A confiture is when you first set the water and sugar to the right consistency (usually jam point or a little higher toward soft-ball on a sugar thermometer) and then add the fruit to the syrup.

  To sterilise glass jars, wash jars and lids in a dishwasher or in hot, soapy water. Rinse thoroughly, then place upside-down on a baking sheet lined with baking paper and dry for 10 minutes in an oven preheated to 160°C (fan)/350°F/Gas 4. Handle with care.

Apricot Jam

Gem de caise

Makes 4 x 200 ml (7 fl oz) jars

1 kg (2 lb 4 oz) apricots
250 g (9 oz/generous 1 cup) jam
   (preserving) sugar
50 ml (1¾ fl oz/3 tablespoons) water
juice of 2 large lemons

Slice the apricots and place them in a jam pan or heavy-duty pan together with the sugar, water and lemon juice. Gently bring to a simmer, stirring often. When the sugar has completely dissolved, increase the heat and simmer for 30 minutes.

Remove from the heat and allow to cool with a wet dish towel on top of the pan, then bring to the boil again and simmer for a further 15 minutes.

Remove from the heat and while it is still warm, carefully pour the mixture into sterilised jars (see opposite), right up to the brim. Seal immediately and consume within a week.

If you are planning to keep the jam for longer, return the jars to a pan full of water, submerge them, bring to the boil and then simmer for 20 minutes. Remove and turn the jars upside down to cool on their lids.

Note

The same method can be used to make peach, plum and damson jam. Add your favourite flavourings.

Blackcurrant and Elderberry Jam

Gem de coacăze negre şi soc

Makes 5 x 250 ml (8½ fl oz) jars

1 kg (2 lb 4 oz) blackcurrants
250 g (9 oz) elderberries
320 g (11 oz/1⅓ cups) jam (preserving) sugar
50 ml (1¾ fl oz/3 tablespoons) water
juice of 2 large lemons

Place all the ingredients in a jam pan or heavy-duty pan and bring to the boil, then reduce the heat and simmer for 40-50 minutes until thick.

Remove from the heat and while it is still warm, carefully pour the mixture into sterilised jars (see opposite), right up to the brim. Seal immediately and consume within a week.

If you are planning to keep the jam for longer, return the jars to a pan full of water, submerge them, bring to the boil and then simmer for 20 minutes. Remove and turn the jars upside down to cool on their lids.

Note

You can use the same method for raspberries, strawberries, blueberries or bilberries.

Sweet Snacks and Gifts

Rose-Petal Confiture

Dulceață de trandafiri

Makes 1 x 100 ml (3½ fl oz) jar

100 g (3½ oz) rose petals
4 tablespoons lemon juice (from fresh lemons)
200 ml (7 fl oz/scant 1 cup) water
180 g (6½ oz/¾ cup) caster (superfine) sugar

In a bowl, rub the rose petals with the lemon juice, crushing them lightly with your fingertips. Set aside.

Bring the water and sugar to the boil in a pan, then simmer until it reaches the consistency of very thin honey. (On a sugar thermometer, it is the soft-ball or jam consistency.) Add the rose petals and simmer until the mixture thickens again.

Remove from the heat and allow to cool.

Pour the confiture into a sterilised jar (see page 260), right up to the brim, and seal.

It will keep for up to 1 year in a cool, dark place.

Note

In Romania, we serve just a teaspoon of this exquisite jam alongside a cup of black coffee and a small glass of water. It is a very special treat, which also makes for a wonderful gift.

Cherry Confiture

Dulceață de cireșe

Makes 4 x 250 ml (8½ fl oz) jars

150 ml (5 fl oz/scant ⅔ cup) water
500 g (1 lb 2 oz/2 generous cups) jam (preserving) sugar
juice of 1 lemon
1 kg (2 lb 4 oz) cherries, pitted

Bring the water and sugar to the boil in a pan, then simmer until it reaches the consistency of very thin honey. (On a sugar thermometer, it is the soft-ball or jam consistency.) Add the lemon juice and fruit and boil for about 20 minutes, removing the foam on top carefully with a slotted spoon.

Remove from the heat and allow to cool. If the syrup is still too thin after cooling, remove the cherries and bring it to the boil again, reducing to the desired consistency. I like my confitures not too thick.

Pour the confiture into sterilised jars (see page 260) right up to the brim and seal.

It will keep for up to 1 year in a cool, dark place.

Note

Use the same method for any type of fruit, including diced pears and cantaloupe.

Candied Citrus Peel

Coajă confiată de citirice

This is a no-recipe type of recipe, meaning that you have the freedom to make any quantity you like whether using orange, lemon or grapefruit peel. I found a recipe for candied lemon peel called *Citronat* in a late 19th-century cookbook, which stored the peel in a jar together with the resulting thickened syrup, from which I adapted the recipe below. It is easier today to store citrus peel in the freezer after having drained it on a rack for a few hours. I eat them as a snack. They also make the perfect edible gift when dipped in chocolate.

Cut your chosen fruit into halves and use a juicer to squeeze out all the juice (you can drink this or make lemonade). Cut the peel into 8 wedges, then remove and discard as much flesh and pith as possible. Slice the peels in half again and transfer to a pan. Pour in enough water to just cover and bring to the boil. Reduce the heat and simmer for 15 minutes with the lid on until the peel starts to soften. If you are using grapefruit peel, taste it and if it's still too bitter, repeat this step once more, simmering for a further 5 minutes.

Strain the mixture over a measuring jug. Make a note of the quantity of liquid, then discard it. Set the peel aside.

In a new pan, add the same quantity of fresh water and sugar in a 50:50 ratio. Let's say you had 200 ml (7 fl oz/scant 1 cup) of liquid, so you add 100 ml (3½ fl oz/scant ½ cup) of fresh water and 100 g (3½ oz/scant ½ cup) of caster sugar. Bring to the boil, then reduce the heat and simmer with the lid off until it starts to thicken slightly. Now add the citrus peel and continue to simmer for at least 40 minutes, or until the syrup falls off the back of a spoon in a continuous stream rather than in drops. On a sugar thermometer, this should be the 'jam consistency' mark.

Transfer the peel to sterilised jars (see page 260) and seal. It will keep in the refrigerator for 1 year, even if you open it to use in desserts.

Note

You can use another storage method if you prefer. Remove the peel from the syrup and drain on a wire cooling rack overnight. Pack the slices into an airtight container or bag and store them in the freezer.

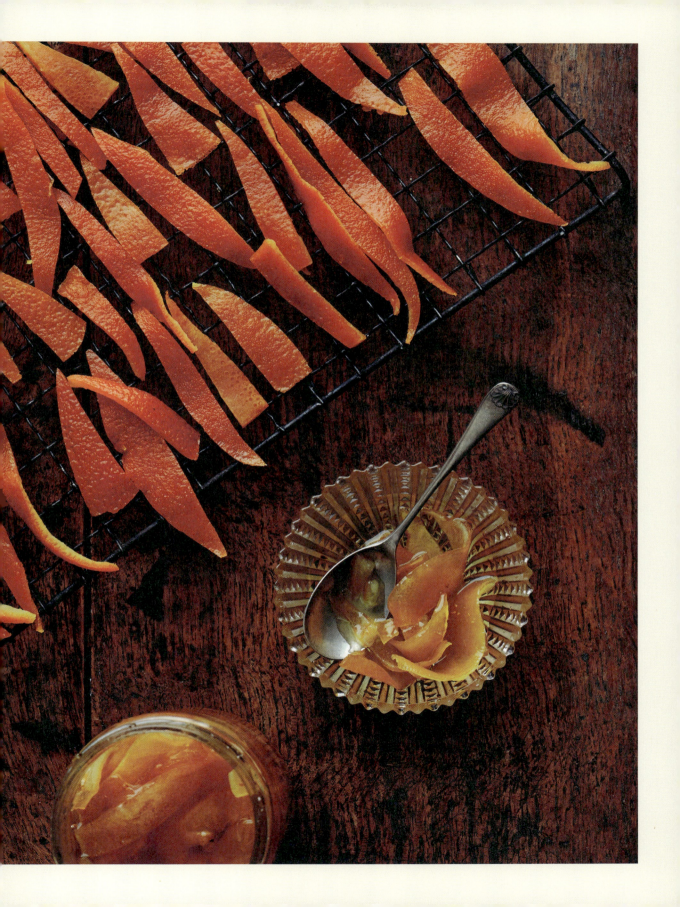

Acknowledgements

I would never have written this book had it not been for the tremendous support of people who showed their faith in me. So here starts my long list of thank yous, with my dear friend Codruţa Cruceanu for her resourcefulness, meticulous project management skills and for keeping my feet on the ground.

While researching the Székelys' land in Transylvania, I was lucky to meet Hunor Boér, librarian at the Székely National Museum in Sf. Gheorghe, and I'll be forever in debt to his generosity, and his time and patience explaining controversial aspects of our history. Through Hunor, I met Katalin Jancso, a passionate food historian who guided me through the forgotten art of making gingerbread and pointed me in the right direction.

The book has taken you on a journey through the Saxon villages in Transylvania, and I was lucky to be able to speak with the founder of their restoration movement, Ms. Caroline Fernolend, who told me about her family recipes. The young team that she is working with at Mihai Eminescu Trust is fiercely proud of the Saxon heritage, and did everything possible to show me around. Special thanks to Michaela Türk, Liza Bunescu, Alexandru Neagu and Alex Avram for preparing the best *papanasi* in town, with the best locally made curd cheese and homemade jam.

Travelling through south-eastern Transylvania, we were welcomed with open arms and some of the best pies and cakes in the region. My gratitude goes to Denisa Babeş for making the famous rhubarb cake with meringue and the curd cheese doughnuts at her guest house, no. 333 in Mălâncrav. Thank you to Sorina Matei Vonu for preparing the iconic Saxon pie called *lichiu*, which you can definitely try if you are staying at Folberth guesthouse in Criţ. Thank you to Mihaela Neagu for her hospitality at 276 Stadtern-Hof guesthouse in Mălâncrav, which we booked through Experience Transylvania, and to our guide Maria, who works as a volunteer for Mihai Eminescu Trust in her spare time. Also to 'auntie' Elena Pascu, who is a traditional embroiderer in Mălâncrav, who spent time with us explaining about traditional patterns and colours.

The book's journey has taken me to Germany, where I was lucky to find the help of Halrun Reinholz from the Banater Schwaben Kulturzentrum in Ulm. I can't be grateful enough to her for sharing all her knowledge, not only in traditional recipes but in history, too. A special thank you goes to Patrick Polling, the leader of Bundesvorsitzender der Deutschen Banater Jugend- und Trachtengruppen in Germany, and to his grandparents Elisabeth and Andreas Schöps who shared their family story with me.

At at time when my research endeavours seemed to take me nowhere, I felt grateful to have found a group of enthusiastic young people working for the Armenian Union in Romania, ready to talk about their favourite baking recipes. I was fortunate enough to meet Paul Agopian, committed to discovering and restoring his Armenian roots and the story of his community. His website, negustorie.ro, is one of the best resources of this kind in Romania.

The journey continued and I couldn't have written the section about the Magyars in Romania without the help of Rebeka Stamate and Lorant Szocs, who generously gave me their time and shared their family recipes with me. The same goes for Katia Pascariu, who helped me write about the Jewish community in Bucharest.

To complement everyone's contributions, I read thousands of pages of history, family stories and food history books. For the latter, I need to mention Daniel Voinea, Librăriile Cărtureşti and GastroArt publishers for their important work in raising awareness and writing about Romania's cuisine, its past and its identity. I would also like to acknowledge the tremendous work carried out by the University Babeş-Bolyai in Cluj Napoca, especially by professor Sorin Mitu, who is among the few in Romania to believe that 'food is culture'. Thank you to numerous museums in Romania for their professionalism in answering random questions sent out of the blue. Special thanks to Dana Hrib at the Brukenthal Museum in Sibiu, who embraced the idea of my book wholeheartedly.

Back in the UK, the team that worked to make this book happen needs a very special thank you, from my publisher Kajal Mistry and my editor Emily Preece-Morrison, to food stylist Joss Herd and her assistant Hattie Arnold, to prop stylist Tabitha Hawkins and photographer Matt Russell. I will be forever grateful to you all.

And to keep things going, I will be publishing guides to where to stay in Transylvania and other regions throughout the country, with links to what to visit and whom to meet, on my website irinageorgescu.com and on social media.

Location photo captions:

page 11: Guesthouse 276 Mălâncrav;
pages 44, 84, 114: Folberth guesthouse in Criţ;
pages 54, 137: Mihai Eminescu Trust Sighişoara;
pages 155, 156, 157, 170: Guesthouse 333 Mălâncrav

Published in 2022 by Hardie Grant Books,
an imprint of Hardie Grant Publishing

Hardie Grant Books (London)
5th & 6th Floors
52–54 Southwark Street
London SE1 1UN

Hardie Grant Books (Melbourne)
Building 1, 658 Church Street
Richmond, Victoria 3121

hardiegrantbooks.com

Additional photo credits:
p.104 Vasilina Sirotina/Unsplash;
p.106 Irina Georgescu; p.224 Saru Robert/Unsplash

British Library Cataloguing-in-Publication Data. A catalogue record
for this book is available from the British Library.

Tava
ISBN: 978-1-78488-544-1

10 9 8 7 6 5 4 3 2

Publishing Director: Kajal Mistry
Project Editor: Emily Preece-Morrison
Design and Illustrations: Evi-O. Studio | Kait Polkinghorne
Photographer: Matt Russell
Food Stylist: Joss Herd, assisted by Hattie Arnold
Prop Stylist: Tabitha Hawkins
Proofreader: Vicky Orchard
Indexer: Vanessa Bird
Production Controller: Nikolaus Ginelli

Colour reproduction by p2d
Printed and bound in China
by Leo Paper Products Ltd.